A TWITTER YEAR

365 days *in* 140 characters

COMPILED BY KATE BUSSMANN

BLOOMSBURY
NEW YORK · BERLIN · LONDON · SYDNEY

To @alexavh, who came up with the idea,
and @robinmciver, who suffered the consequences

First published in 2011

Copyright © 2011 by Kate Bussmann
Text of tweets © individual tweeters

Twitter is a trademark of Twitter, Inc.
and is used with the permission of Twitter, Inc.

Published by Bloomsbury USA, New York

All papers used by Bloomsbury USA are natural, recyclable products made
from wood grown in well-managed forests. The manufacturing processes
conform to the environmental regulations of the country of origin.

Every reasonable effort has been made to trace copyright holders of
material reproduced in this book, but if any have been inadvertently
overlooked the publishers would be glad to hear from them. For legal
purposes the list of acknowledgements on pp. 275–80 constitutes
an extension of this copyright page.

Bloomsbury USA, 175 Fifth Ave., New York, NY 10010

www.bloomsburyusa.com

LIBRARY OF CONGRESS CATALOGING-IN-PUBLICATION DATA HAS BEEN APPLIED FOR.

ISBN 978-1-60819-903-7

10 9 8 7 6 5 4 3 2 1

Designed and typeset by seagulls.net

Printed in the United States of America by Quad/Graphics,
Fairfield, Pennsylvania

— Contents —

INTRO

POLITICS &
CURRENT AFFAIRS

ROYALTY &
RELIGION

CELEBRITY

SCIENCE &
NATURE

SPORT &
LEISURE

ARTS, CULTURE
& MEDIA

A TWEET A DAY

GLOSSARY
& THANKS

— Introduction —

In 2011, Twitter came of age. You don't even need to have visited the website to know that: tweets are now routinely quoted in newspapers and on television, and hashtags and usernames have started to appear where websites and email addresses used to go. Over the past 12 months, it's made plenty of headlines of its own too, most notably for the way it helped revolutionaries in the Arab world spread the word about atrocities and upcoming demonstrations. It's so pervasive, in fact, that it's hard to believe that the website is only five years old.

The brainchild of American software expert Jack Dorsey, Twitter was originally conceived simply as a way to share short messages with friends. Dorsey sent the first tweet on 21 March 2006, and the full version rolled out to the public

65million
Average number of tweets sent
per day, June 2010

230million
Average number of tweets sent
per day, September 2011

Source: Twitter

INTRO

POLITICS &
CURRENT AFFAIRS

ROYALTY &
RELIGION

CELEBRITY

SCIENCE &
NATURE

SPORT &
LEISURE

ARTS, CULTURE
& MEDIA

A TWEET A DAY

GLOSSARY
& THANKS

on 15 July that year. For a long time it was dismissed as irrelevant; an unnecessary equivalent of the 'status update' feature in Facebook. Gradually, however, it proved itself far more useful than anyone could have predicted. The brevity of a tweet, maximum 140 characters, lends itself neatly to headlines and reportage of fast-moving events. Even if you don't tweet yourself, you can use it as a news aggregator, following any individual or organisation you're interested in, or searching by subject using hashtags. The retweet function means that news and information is easily and quickly disseminated. The cleverly simple way that an @ symbol allows you to communicate with any other user on Twitter means not only that conversations are easily struck up between strangers, but that fans can speak directly to their idols, and voters to their elected representatives. And that 140-character limit makes it a perfect format for pithy remarks – which explains why comedians are amongst the most followed – but perhaps surprisingly, it is also often enough to convey a great deal of emotion.

Those of us who use it – and our numbers are increasing at an astonishing rate – know that more and more, news breaks first on Twitter, from the long-awaited capture of Osama Bin Laden to the untimely death of Amy Winehouse. We log in to follow unfolding events in real time, reading instant reports from the ground and incisive and funny commentary by our friends and experts. This book seeks to capture and curate the sharpest observations and the best of that reportage. At the end, you'll find a chronological précis of the whole year, crowd-sourced tweet by tweet. In the chapters that follow this introduction, there are in-depth 'live-tweet' descriptions of the biggest events of the year, punctuated with illustrative statistics and lists of the most popular Twitter users in their field. But, as your parents no doubt told you, popularity isn't everything: you don't have to have as many followers as Lady Gaga to influence the conversation. And this year, plenty of us did just that.

456
Peak TPS when Michael Jackson died on 25 June 2009

8,868
Peak TPS when Beyoncé Knowles revealed her pregnancy bump at the MTV VMAs, 28 August 2011

Source: Twitter

NUMBER OF TWITTER EMPLOYEES

Jan 2008: 8

Jan 2009: 29

Jan 2010: 130

Jan 2011: 350

Aug 2011: 600

Source: Twitter

INTRO
POLITICS & CURRENT AFFAIRS
ROYALTY & RELIGION
CELEBRITY
SCIENCE & NATURE
SPORT & LEISURE
ARTS, CULTURE & MEDIA
A TWEET A DAY
GLOSSARY & THANKS

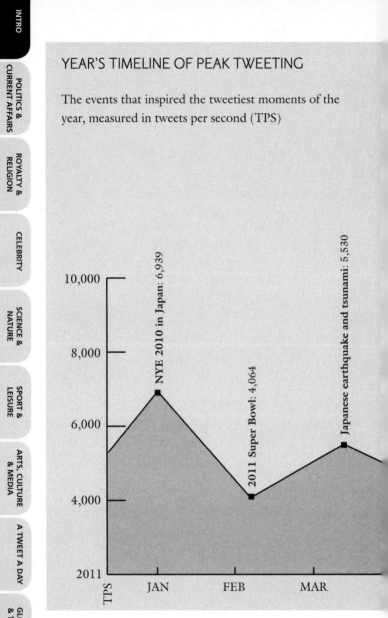

YEAR'S TIMELINE OF PEAK TWEETING

The events that inspired the tweetiest moments of the year, measured in tweets per second (TPS)

NYE 2010 in Japan: 6,939

2011 Super Bowl: 4,064

Japanese earthquake and tsunami: 5,530

10,000

8,000

6,000

4,000

2011

TPS   JAN   FEB   MAR

INTRO

POLITICS & CURRENT AFFAIRS

ROYALTY & RELIGION

CELEBRITY

SCIENCE & NATURE

SPORT & LEISURE

ARTS, CULTURE & MEDIA

A TWEET A DAY

GLOSSARY & THANKS

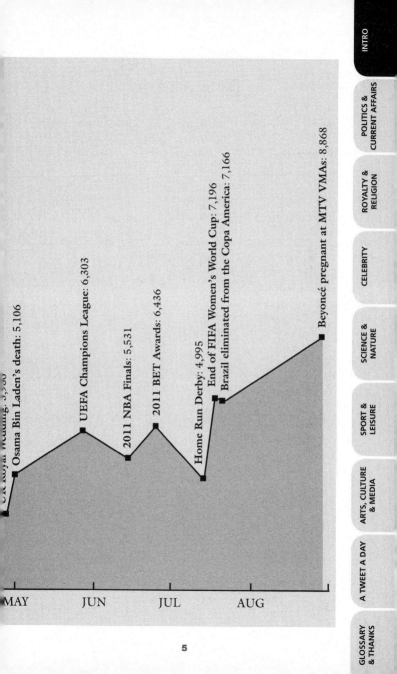

UK Royal Wedding: 3,760

Osama Bin Laden's death: 5,106

UEFA Champions League: 6,303

2011 NBA Finals: 5,531

2011 BET Awards: 6,436

Home Run Derby: 4,995
End of FIFA Women's World Cup: 7,196
Brazil eliminated from the Copa America: 7,166

Beyoncé pregnant at MTV VMAs: 8,868

MAY | JUN | JUL | AUG

INTRO

POLITICS &
CURRENT AFFAIRS

ROYALTY &
RELIGION

CELEBRITY

SCIENCE &
NATURE

SPORT &
LEISURE

ARTS, CULTURE
& MEDIA

A TWEET A DAY

GLOSSARY
& THANKS

INTRO

POLITICS &
CURRENT AFFAIRS

ROYALTY &
RELIGION

CELEBRITY

SCIENCE &
NATURE

SPORT &
LEISURE

ARTS, CULTURE
& MEDIA

A TWEET A DAY

GLOSSARY
& THANKS

The Most Influential
Twitter Accounts

TWEETER	USERNAME	INFLUENCE*	FOLLOWERS
Funny Or Die, sketch comedy website	@funnyordie	96%	2,353,472
Sports Center, TV show on ESPN	@sportscenter	95.6%	1,288,882
Ezra Klein, journalist	@ezraklein	95.4%	95,516
Fast Company, business, technology & design magazine	@fastcompany	95.3%	365,171
Sky News Newsdesk, UK TV channel	@skynewsbreak	95%	340,978
Pitchfork, music news website	@pitchforkmedia	94.7%	1,713,252
Lord Voldemort, character from Harry Potter books	@lord_voldemort7	94.7%	1,593,867
Raditya Dika, Indonesian writer	@radityadika	94.4%	920,442
Darren Rovell, sports/business writer for CNBC	@darrenrovell	94.0%	115,492
Gawker, media website	@gawker	93.7%	111,578

*See Glossary

The Most-followed Twitter Accounts

TWEETER	USERNAME	INFLUENCE	FOLLOWERS
Lady Gaga, musician	@ladygaga	83.8%	12,948,132
Justin Bieber, musician	@justinbieber	74.2%	12,164,201
Barack Obama, politician	@barackobama	83.9%	9,825,149
Katy Perry, musician	@katyperry	82.8%	9,389,630
Kim Kardashian, reality TV star	@kimkardashian	85.7%	9,321,082
Britney Spears, musician	@britneyspears	75.9%	9,188,247
Shakira, musician	@shakira	60.2%	7,943,258
Taylor Swift, musician	@taylorswift13	59.6%	7,684,470
Ashton Kutcher, actor	@aplusk	79.7%	7,493,535
The Ellen Show, TV programme	@theellenshow	68.5%	7,409,502

— Editorial note —

All the tweets in this book are replicated as you'd see them on Twitter: grammar and spelling have *not* been corrected, and where there are multiple variations on a name (e.g. Gaddafi/Qadhafi), they are left as they were originally typed.

When it came to deciding which events to focus on with dedicated 'live-tweet' sections, some major news, cultural and sports stories were obvious choices.

POLITICS & CURRENT AFFAIRS

ROYALTY & RELIGION

CELEBRITY

SCIENCE & NATURE

SPORT & LEISURE

ARTS, CULTURE & MEDIA

A TWEET A DAY

GLOSSARY & THANKS

INTRO

POLITICS &
CURRENT AFFAIRS

ROYALTY &
RELIGION

CELEBRITY

SCIENCE &
NATURE

SPORT &
LEISURE

ARTS, CULTURE
& MEDIA

A TWEET A DAY

GLOSSARY
& THANKS

Some were events that provoked a lot of conversation and jokes on Twitter. A third set were incidents that may have been mainly of interest to a small group of people, but involved Twitter itself in one way or another; the story of Cory Booker, Mayor of Newark, using the site to find people who needed help in the aftermath of a blizzard, is one such example.

Any regular user of Twitter will notice that this book does not read like the average timeline: retweets have mainly been avoided, and there are very few @ replies. Excluding 'A Tweet a Day', the section of this book that gives you an overview of the entire year, tweets that link to news stories or pictures have also largely been ignored. Instead the focus is on the commentary, observation and humour that the Twitterverse is so good at.

With a few exceptions, the tweets chosen were originally written in English. This was for the sake of simplicity, but the focus throughout has nonetheless remained as much as possible on first-hand witnesses of, say, the events in Tahrir Square or the Japanese earthquake. In a few cases, however, an exception was made to this rule: you won't find the tweets sent by children on Utøya island desperately seeking help, nor the ones sent later by parents trying to find the missing.

IMPORTANT

- The year in this book runs from October 2010 to September 2011.
- Twitter constantly updates its statistics. Those given in the book are accurate at the time of compilation.

— 1 —

POLITICS & CURRENT AFFAIRS

@Sandmonkey Mahmoud Salem
Good morning Egypt! Today you are free! :) #jan25
9.14 a.m. 12 Feb

INTRO

POLITICS &
CURRENT AFFAIRS

ROYALTY &
RELIGION

CELEBRITY

SCIENCE &
NATURE

SPORT &
LEISURE

ARTS, CULTURE
& MEDIA

A TWEET A DAY

GLOSSARY
& THANKS

The Most-followed ___ Political Leaders

TWEETER	USERNAME	FOLLOWERS
Barack Obama, President of the USA	@barackobama	9,825,149
Al Gore, former vice-president of the USA	@algore	2,275,070
Dalai Lama, political leader of Tibet	@dalailama	2,255,979
Arnold Schwarzenegger, former governor of California	@Schwarzenegger	2,106,515
David Cameron, Prime Minister of Great Britain	@Number10gov	1,834,678
John McCain, US senator	@senjohnmccain	1,733,711
Newt Gingrich, Republican candidate (2012) for President of the USA	@NewtGingrich	1,327,541
Gavin Newsom, Lieutenant-Governor of California	@GavinNewsom	1,301,083
Shashi Tharoor, Member of Parliament, India	@shashitharoor	1,119,828
Cory Booker, Mayor of Newark, New Jersey	@CoryBooker	1,094,198
Kevin Rudd, Prime Minister of Australia	@kruddmp	996,483
Sarah Palin, Republican candidate for vice-president of the USA	@SarahPalin	641,670

INTRO

POLITICS &
CURRENT AFFAIRS

ROYALTY &
RELIGION

CELEBRITY

SCIENCE &
NATURE

SPORT &
LEISURE

ARTS, CULTURE
& MEDIA

A TWEET A DAY

GLOSSARY
& THANKS

Politics &
Current Affairs

There are those who rightly scoff at the idea that the Arab Spring couldn't have happened without Twitter or Facebook. The anger and frustration behind the revolutions that toppled one dictator after another was bubbling long before either even existed. What is without question is that social media helped rebels organise faster and more easily than ever before, just as it helped communities turn outrage into positive action in the wake of the London riots. Both were organised without the help of traditional media, and both embody the Twitterverse's anarchic streak that on multiple occasions this year has put politicians (and a litigious Welsh striker) on the back foot. It can bring people together in the worst of times, but also the best.

INTRO

POLITICS &
CURRENT AFFAIRS

ROYALTY &
RELIGION

CELEBRITY

SCIENCE &
NATURE

SPORT &
LEISURE

ARTS, CULTURE
& MEDIA

A TWEET A DAY

GLOSSARY
& THANKS

— 12 OCTOBER 2010 —

RESCUE OF THE CHILEAN MINERS

The story began on 5 August, when the roof of the main entrance to a copper mine in Copiapó, Chile, collapsed. On 22 August a rescue probe that had drilled over 2,000 feet down made contact with the trapped miners, who sent back the message, 'All 33 of us are well inside the shelter'. Three holes were sunk simultaneously and on 9 October a drill broke through to the men. Once the shaft was lined with metal and deemed safe, the rescue began.

Note: All times local to Copiapó, Chile

— Who's Who —

SEBASTIAN PIÑERA: Chile's president – @sebastianpinera
LAURENCE GOLBORNE: Chile's mining minister – @lgolborne

@reuters_tlw reuters peru tlw
Manuel Gonzalez is the first rescuer. Pressure is on. He will go down the equivalent of 200 storey building.
#chileanminers #rescatemineros
11.13 p.m. 12 Oct

@indiaknight India Knight
Oh my god. Wake up! Put tv on! Incredible footage.
11.36 p.m. 12 Oct

12

@rorycarroll72 Rory Carroll
Capsule landed, miners embracing manuel gonzalez.
Families erupt.
11.39 p.m. 12 Oct

@sebastianpinera Sebastian Piñera
Que emocion! Que felicidad! Que orgullo de ser Chileno!
Y que gratitud con Dios!
[*What emotion! What happiness! What Chilean pride!
And what gratitude to God!*]
11.52 p.m. 12 Oct

@SantiagoTimes The Santiago Times
First of the 33 miners, Florencio Avalos, has reached the
surface and is out of the capsule. Avalos embraces his
emotional wife and son
12.12 a.m. 13 Oct

@indiaknight India Knight
* hands out tissues* Here, blow.
12.14 a.m. 13 Oct

@SarahBrownUK Sarah Brown
assume everyone everywhere is as distracted as me, from
whatever they are doing, by the hourly rescue of each
Chilean miner #rescatemineros
8.08 a.m. 13 Oct

@daffodilfairy vikki
Managed 5 minutes of work but now been sidetacked
by Chilean Miners again!! Will Power? Me? No, I don't
think so!!
8.28 a.m. 13 Oct

13

INTRO

POLITICS &
CURRENT AFFAIRS

ROYALTY &
RELIGION

CELEBRITY

SCIENCE &
NATURE

SPORT &
LEISURE

ARTS, CULTURE
& MEDIA

A TWEET A DAY

GLOSSARY
& THANKS

@davidvitty Dave Vitty
Miner 21 Yonni Barrios is in the capsule & heading up to
meet his mistress! The wife is understandably narked &
staying at home.
4.28 p.m. 13 Oct

@KatyKatopodis Katy Katopodis
Oh I'm loving the Yonni Barios rescue.
Not sure he looks happy to be out
though. Sky news: "a kiss rather
than a slap in the face". Lol!
4.40 p.m. 13 Oct

@rorycarroll72 Rory Carroll
Obama, the Pope, NASA, media, Chavez, Evo Morales..
everyone praising Sebastian Piñera. If his head expands
any more that helmet will crack.
7.39 p.m. 13 Oct

@GoodnightMouse Rochelle Killiner
Just watching the Chilean miners rescue on CNN. Only
5 men to go. Amazing scenes... need way more tissues!
8.03 p.m. 13 Oct

@HalaGorani Hala Gorani
Ariel Ticona (#32) - who became a father to baby
Esperanza while trapped - is out. Only one man left.
#chilemine
9.34 p.m. 13 Oct

@Karen_DaviLa Karen Davila
Chilean miner Luis Urzua redefines "hero". Kept miners together and chose to be the last miner out.
10.11 p.m. 13 Oct

@rorycarroll72 Rory Carroll
He's out. Not a dry eye in the plaza. Everyone belting out the national anthem.
10.59 p.m. 13 Oct

@lgolborne Laurence Golborne
Subió último rescatista.Ahora podemos decir:el equipo de trabajo,junto a todo el país, rescató a nuestros 33 mineros en 70 días. Lo hicimos!
[*Last rescuer up. Now we can say that our team, along with the whole country, rescued 33 miners in 70 days. We did it!*]
12.32 p.m. 14 Oct

37%
News links on Twitter that related to the rescue, 11–15 October

Source: Pew Research Center's Project for Excellence in Journalism

INTRO

POLITICS &
CURRENT AFFAIRS

ROYALTY &
RELIGION

CELEBRITY

SCIENCE &
NATURE

SPORT &
LEISURE

ARTS, CULTURE
& MEDIA

A TWEET A DAY

GLOSSARY
& THANKS

Liu Xiaobo Wins the Nobel Peace Prize

On 8 October the imprisoned Chinese author and academic Liu Xiaobo won the 2010 Nobel Peace Prize for what the committee described as his 'long and non-violent struggle for fundamental human rights in China'. Two days later his wife, Liu Xia, reacted on Twitter:

@liuxia64 liuxia
兄弟们，我回来了，八号我就被软禁了，不知何时见到大家，我的手机被搞坏，我无法接打电话。见过晓波，监狱在9号晚告诉他得奖的消息。以后的事慢慢说。请大家帮我推。谢谢
[*Brothers, I'm back. On the 8th I was put under house arrest, so I don't know when I'll see you. My phone has been broken and can't take calls. I saw Xiaobo; the prison told him the news of his prize on the night of 9th. Everything else, I'll tell you later. Please give me your support. Thank you*]
10 Oct

Crime and Punishment

13 OCTOBER 2010: Greater Manchester Police decide to post details of every 999 call over a 24-hour period to illustrate how much of their time is taken up by incidents

they describe as 'social work'. In total, 3,205 tweets were sent out, including one detailing a call from a woman who had put the wrong fuel in her car and had decided to abandon it at a petrol station. The move proved popular: their followers rose from 3,000 to 14,000.

— 2 NOVEMBER 2010 —

UNITED STATES MIDTERM ELECTIONS

Halfway through President Barack Obama's term in office, the Democratic Party suffered a major blow, losing control of the House of Representatives to the Republicans; their majority in the Senate was also weakened. The major issues were Obama's controversial health care reforms and the state of the economy. The Tea Party movement also saw its influence increase. Two losers captured Twitter's imagination: former eBay CEO Meg Whitman, who ran for Governor of California, and Christine O'Donnell, Tea Partier and would-be senator for New York, who believed masturbation was a sin, but once admitted to a youthful dalliance with witchcraft.

Note: All times local to Washington DC

@RobReynoldsAJE Rob Reynolds
Christine O'Donnell made an ad assuring voters she was not a witch... now she won't be a Senator either.
7.13 p.m. 2 Nov

INTRO

POLITICS & CURRENT AFFAIRS

ROYALTY & RELIGION

CELEBRITY

SCIENCE & NATURE

SPORT & LEISURE

ARTS, CULTURE & MEDIA

A TWEET A DAY

GLOSSARY & THANKS

INTRO

POLITICS &
CURRENT AFFAIRS

ROYALTY &
RELIGION

CELEBRITY

SCIENCE &
NATURE

SPORT &
LEISURE

ARTS, CULTURE
& MEDIA

A TWEET A DAY

GLOSSARY
& THANKS

@TVDoneWright Adam Wright
Christine O'Donnell losing tonight is a valuable lesson to politicians. Never ever mess with the pro-masturbation vote.
7.29 p.m. 2 Nov

@domknight dominic knight
As Christine O'Donnell lost, she almost certainly isn't a witch. However it may be worth drowning her to make sure.
8.03 p.m. 2 Nov

@mdowney Mike Downey
How could over 93,000 people cast a vote for Christine O'Donnell? She's completely nuts! She lost by a landslide but, still...
8.12 p.m. 2 Nov

@darthvader Darth Vader
If you really want to vote an incumbent out of power, try tossing them down a reactor shaft. Works wonders.
9.04 p.m. 2 Nov

@vegancto Nick Wilson
Meg Whitman just realised that California didn't have a "Buy it Now" button...
10.13 p.m. 2 Nov

@Tribrix Lenny Timons

Guess what? I'm not a witch and I'm not the Senator elect from Delaware. That's two things I have in common with Christine O'Donnell!

12.40 a.m. 3 Nov

@B_Hay Brendan Hay
Meg Whitman spent $160 million on her gubernatorial run and lost. I assume because Jerry Brown bid $161 million during the 30 seconds.
9.07 a.m. 3 Nov

@joshgerstein Josh Gerstein
It's not a "thumpin'" he took. It's a "shellacking," Obama says. #Whbrief
12.56 p.m. 3 Nov

@Ted_Newton Ted Newton
Shellac is made out of slimy bug spit. So, #shellacking sounds about right...
1.18 p.m. 3 Nov

@SageFrancis Sage Francis
The Tea Party hasn't delivered on ANY of their promises yet. WHAT GIVES???
2.49 p.m. 3 Nov

INTRO

POLITICS &
CURRENT AFFAIRS

ROYALTY &
RELIGION

CELEBRITY

SCIENCE &
NATURE

SPORT &
LEISURE

ARTS, CULTURE
& MEDIA

A TWEET A DAY

GLOSSARY
& THANKS

MIDTERM TWEETS

Average number of tweets sent during the campaign by the 687 candidates running for national House, Senate and gubernatorial seats.

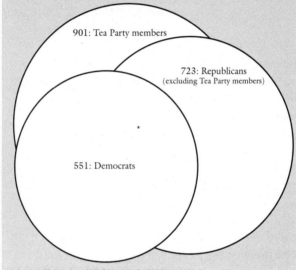

901: Tea Party members

723: Republicans
(excluding Tea Party members)

551: Democrats

Source: University of Michigan study, 2011

22%

Online Americans who talked about the midterms on Twitter or another social networking site

Source: Pew Internet and American Life Report

INTRO

POLITICS & CURRENT AFFAIRS

ROYALTY & RELIGION

CELEBRITY

SCIENCE & NATURE

SPORT & LEISURE

ARTS, CULTURE & MEDIA

A TWEET A DAY

GLOSSARY & THANKS

___ The Top Terms Used by Candidates ___
during the Midterm Elections

DEMOCRATS	REPUBLICANS (NON-TEA PARTY)	TEA PARTY
education	spending	barney_frank
jobs	bill	conservative
oil_spill	budget	tea_party
clean_energy	wsj [*Wall Street Journal*]	clinton
afghanistan	bush	nancy_pelosi
reform	deficit	obamacare

Source: University of Michigan study, 2011

— 28 NOVEMBER 2010 —
WIKILEAKS RELEASE SECRET DIPLOMATIC CABLES

The underground organisation WikiLeaks released their latest cache of secret documents: over 250,000 classified cables sent from American embassies, including personal critiques of foreign leaders, enemies and allies alike. A diplomatic storm ensued, and the hunt for Julian Assange, WikiLeaks' leader-in-hiding, intensified. Meanwhile, the hacking collective Anonymous began attacking the websites of corporations, including Mastercard, for allegedly bowing to political pressure and refusing to handle donations to WikiLeaks.

Note: All times local to Washington DC

INTRO

POLITICS &
CURRENT AFFAIRS

ROYALTY &
RELIGION

CELEBRITY

SCIENCE &
NATURE

SPORT &
LEISURE

ARTS, CULTURE
& MEDIA

A TWEET A DAY

GLOSSARY
& THANKS

@evgenymorozov Evgeny Morozov
WikiLeaks is what happens when the entire US
government is forced to go through a full-body scanner
12.31 p.m. 28 Nov

@fionndavenport Fionn Davenport
Wikileaks reveals US officials refer to Sarkozy as 'the
emperor with no clothes.' Now THAT'S funny. #wikileaks
2.35 p.m. 28 Nov

@rickjnewman Rick Newman
Biggest #Wikileaks disappointment: No pix of Qadaffi's
#voluptuousblonde Ukrainian nurse. And Google
search a bust.
9.41 p.m. 29 Nov

@marykissel Mary Kissel
Best #wikileaks quote: Lee Kuan Yew on Kim Jong Il.
A "'flabby old chap' for a leader who prances around
stadiums seeking adulation."
8.16 a.m. 30 Nov

@yapdates Conrade
"WikiLeaks" stems from a misguided sense of 'freedom
of speech.' What's private and confidential must remain
private and confidential.
7.40 p.m. 30 Nov

@mulegirl Erika Hall
78%: The proportion of Americans who think that
WikiLeaks and Wikipedia are owned by the same
company.
10.16 a.m. 8 Dec

INTRO

POLITICS &
CURRENT AFFAIRS

ROYALTY &
RELIGION

CELEBRITY

SCIENCE &
NATURE

SPORT &
LEISURE

ARTS, CULTURE
& MEDIA

A TWEET A DAY

GLOSSARY
& THANKS

@mikestaszel Mike Staszel

*Condoms: $5. 2 dinners and a movie: $150.
Train ticket out of town: $40. Anonymous
taking down MasterCard.com: Priceless.*

#wikileaks
10.24 a.m. 8 Dec

@katiecouric Katie Couric
Funny quote in light of wikileaks: "gvmt should
sometimes be shrouded for same reason middle-aged
people should be clothed." William Galston
3.44 p.m. 16 Dec

— 8 JANUARY 2011 —
THE TUCSON SHOOTING

During a public meeting held by US Representative Gabrielle Giffords in a supermarket car park in Tucson, Arizona,
a gunman opened fire on the crowd. Six people were
killed, including a nine-year-old girl. Giffords was shot
in the head but survived. Local man Jared Loughner was
arrested and charged with the crimes and a debate began
about whether the extreme tone of some political debate
was in any way to blame. Liberals levelled criticism at Sarah
Palin, whose Facebook page had published a map of the
USA with crosshairs indicating Democrats who had voted
for the health care bill; Giffords was one of them.

Note: All times local to Tucson, Arizona

INTRO

POLITICS &
CURRENT AFFAIRS

ROYALTY &
RELIGION

CELEBRITY

SCIENCE &
NATURE

SPORT &
LEISURE

ARTS, CULTURE
& MEDIA

A TWEET A DAY

GLOSSARY
& THANKS

@markos Markos Moulitsas
Mission accomplished, Sarah Palin, http://is.gd/knNgl
11.19 a.m. 8 Jan

@MattBinder Matt Binder
We've seen what Sarah Palin's
Alaska looks like. The shooting of
Rep Gabrielle Giffords today gives a
preview Sarah Palin's America.
1.07 p.m. 8 Jan

@billhuizenga Bill Huizenga
Prayers go out to the family of Rep Gabrielle Giffords
(AZ) who was shot earlier today. Conflicting reports of
her status, so please pray.
1.17 p.m. 8 Jan

@AndrewBreitbart AndrewBreitbart
Of those who're now using this tragedy 4 political
purposes, what's your proof of this lunatic's motivation?
Isn't that majorly relevant?
1.43 p.m. 8 Jan

@caitieparker Caitie Parker
Official I went to high school & college, & was in a band
w/ the gunman. I can't even fathom this right now.
2.06 p.m. 8 Jan

@caitieparker Caitie Parker
@antderosa As I knew him he was left wing, quite liberal.
& oddly obsessed with the 2012 prophecy.
2.26 p.m. 8 Jan

INTRO

POLITICS &
CURRENT AFFAIRS

ROYALTY &
RELIGION

CELEBRITY

SCIENCE &
NATURE

SPORT &
LEISURE

ARTS, CULTURE
& MEDIA

A TWEET A DAY

GLOSSARY
& THANKS

@GovMikeHuckabee Gov. Mike Huckabee
Please join Janet and me in praying for Congresswoman
Gabrielle Giffords and all the victims of the tragic
shooting in Arizona.
2.45 p.m. 8 Jan

@jstrevino Joshua Treviño
@ayeletw It's important to proceed from evidence.
The Giffords shooter appears to be a mentally ill
conspiratorialist -- not a Republican.
3.10 p.m. 8 Jan

@MelissaTweets Melissa Clouthier
LAT reporter first question: Do you know shooter's
motives? Ans: No. #Giffords
11.09 a.m. 9 Jan

@jimgeraghty jimgeraghty
Among the politicians who have featured pictures of
themselves aiming guns at targets: Gabrielle Giffords.
http://flic.kr/p/6X2Ao8
7.12 a.m. 10 Jan

3rd

This was the third biggest story
on Twitter in a single week
since Jan 2007

*Source: Pew Research
Center's Project for
Excellence in Journalism*

3:1

Ratio of critical to supportive tweets
and blogs about Giffords,
8–16 January

25

Source: Crimson Hexagon

INTRO

POLITICS & CURRENT AFFAIRS

ROYALTY & RELIGION

CELEBRITY

SCIENCE & NATURE

SPORT & LEISURE

ARTS, CULTURE & MEDIA

A TWEET A DAY

GLOSSARY & THANKS

@astroboh Brian O'Halloran
'Blood libel', @SarahPalinUSA? Oh dear, oh dear.
You didn't think that one through, did you? #giffords
7.38 a.m. 12 Jan

— 11 FEBRUARY 2011 —

MUBARAK STANDS DOWN

Inspired by the Tunisian demonstrations that succeeded in ousting 23-year dictator Zine el-Abidine Ben Ali from power on 14 January, ordinary Egyptians began to realise they might be able to do the same. Beginning on 25 January, thousands of protesters flocked to the aptly named Tahrir [liberation] Square calling for the resignation of Hosni Mubarak, who had been president for four decades. The government responded with violence that left more than 300 people dead. They also shut down access to social media networks, including Twitter (which protesters were using to organise), mobile phone networks and all Internet service providers, bar the one used by the stock exchange. Protesters managed to tweet anyway, by calling in messages to friends abroad or trading an interview with foreign media for time on their satellite links. On 10 February Mubarak ceded all power to Vice-President Omar Suleiman, but insisted he would remain to the end of his term. For the people on the streets, that was not enough.

Note: All times local to Cairo, Egypt

@ircpresident Mohamed ElGohary
Those who are going to Tahrir, no need, #Tahrir has now more than enough. Go to the Presidential palace #Jan25
1.47 p.m. 11 Feb

@BreakingNews Breaking News
Report: Mubarak has left for the United Arab Emirates - Al Jazeera http://read.bi/dH9j7I
3.22 p.m. 11 Feb

@3arabawy Hossam ومع ماسح
protesters in Tahrir r flying kites on high altitudes to harass the military helicopter :D #jan25
4.59 p.m. 11 Feb

@TerryMoran Terry Moran
#Egypt: Army tanks slowly turn their turrets away from the crowd at palace. A soldier in one of the tanks takes a flag and starts waving it.
5.14 p.m. 11 Feb

@acarvin Andy Carvin
Evening prayer taking place in Tahrir. Always a marvel to watch. #jan25
5.59 p.m. 11 Feb

@ianinegypt Ian James Lee
Mubarak steps down to Allahu Akbar ringing out in Tahrir Square. #egypt #jan25
6.03 p.m. 11 Feb

INTRO

POLITICS & CURRENT AFFAIRS

ROYALTY & RELIGION

CELEBRITY

SCIENCE & NATURE

SPORT & LEISURE

ARTS, CULTURE & MEDIA

A TWEET A DAY

GLOSSARY & THANKS

INTRO

POLITICS &
CURRENT AFFAIRS

ROYALTY &
RELIGION

CELEBRITY

SCIENCE &
NATURE

SPORT &
LEISURE

ARTS, CULTURE
& MEDIA

A TWEET A DAY

GLOSSARY
& THANKS

@Zeinobia Zeinobia

The army council is ruling the country now , I got tears in my eyes , we are free , yes we are free
6.04 p.m. 11 Feb

@mkanders Mark Anderson
Nov. 9, 1989. I still remember, vividly, watching TV news in awe as Berlin Wall came down. Same, I think, w/ #AlJazeera images today. #Egypt
6.35 p.m. 11 Feb

@Sandmonkey Mahmoud Salem
FIREWORKS, CELEBRATIONS, FUN! JUBILATION! I AM NOT MAKING SENSE. I AM HEADING TO TAHRIR! #JAN25
6.57 p.m. 11 Feb

@Sandmonkey Mahmoud Salem
To everyone who rediculed us, opposed us, wanted us to compromise, i say: YOU ARE WELCOME :) TODAY WE ALL CELEBRATE!!! #JAN25
6.58 p.m. 11 Feb

@jonsnowC4 Jon Snow
Ecstacy on Tahrir square..central Cairo awash with 100,000's rejoicing: no resistance:the army so far soft, relaxed promising free elections
7.03 p.m. 11 Feb

COUNTRIES TWEETING ABOUT EGYPT ON 28 JAN

At midnight on 28 January, protesters suffered a violent backlash from the police and Mubarak loyalists. Guns, tear gas, water cannon and rubber bullets were fired into crowds, and hundreds across the country died.

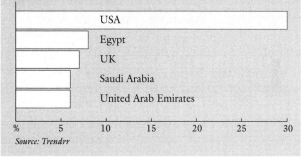

Source: Trendrr

@EvanHD Evan Davis
In future peaceful revolutions, demonstrators will keep at it for at least 18 days now they know that perseverance pays. Dictators beware
7.43 p.m. 11 Feb

@lindseyhilsum Lindsey Hilsum
This is the most fun I've had reporting for @channel4news in ages. What a story #egypt!
9.19 p.m. 11 Feb

@Zeinobia Zeinobia
congrats to Egypt , to the Arab world to the free world, we have won our battle :) still our war for better Egypt is still on
12.18 a.m. 12 Feb

INTRO

POLITICS & CURRENT AFFAIRS

ROYALTY & RELIGION

CELEBRITY

SCIENCE & NATURE

SPORT & LEISURE

ARTS, CULTURE & MEDIA

A TWEET A DAY

GLOSSARY & THANKS

INTRO

POLITICS &
CURRENT AFFAIRS

ROYALTY &
RELIGION

CELEBRITY

SCIENCE &
NATURE

SPORT &
LEISURE

ARTS, CULTURE
& MEDIA

A TWEET A DAY

GLOSSARY
& THANKS

@Sandmonkey Mahmoud Salem

Good morning Egypt! Today you are free! :) #jan25

9.14 a.m. 12 Feb

— Crime and Punishment —

21 March 2011: When a laptop belonging to California-based graphic designer Joshua Kaufman was stolen from his apartment, he reported it to police, but, he says, they were unable to properly investigate due to lack of resources. Cleverly, he'd installed an app called Hidden, which allowed him to watch remotely through his computer's webcam and see the computer screen itself. He began posting images on his blog (thisguyhasmymacbook.tumblr.com) of the person who was using it, spread the word through Twitter and on 31 May police arrested the man in the pictures. Kaufman got his computer back the following day.

— Tweeting Without Thinking —

25 March 2011: Dutch politician Frank van der Vorst accidentally tweeted a message that was intended as a DM, which translates thus: 'As you throbbingly climax for the first time I feel your juices in my mouth as if they were the nectar of love.' To his credit, the unmarried politician took the embarrassment well, tweeting later about the number of followers he'd gained.

— 2 MAY 2011 —

OSAMA BIN LADEN KILLED

By the time Barack Obama announced that the leader of al-Qaeda had been assassinated by US forces in the town of Abbottabad, Pakistan, Twitter had already broken the story. The operation had in fact been live-tweeted by IT consultant Sohaib Athar, who was unaware at the time of what he was witnessing.

Note: All times local to Pakistan. Although Obama made his announcement on 1 May, in Pakistan it was already 2 May when Sohaib Athar was live-tweeting the events there. The latter date is therefore cited above and below.

@ReallyVirtual Sohaib Athar
Helicopter hovering above Abbottabad at 1AM (is a rare event).
12.58 a.m. 2 May

@ReallyVirtual Sohaib Athar
Go away helicopter - before I take out my giant swatter :-/
1.05 a.m. 2 May

@ReallyVirtual Sohaib Athar
A huge window shaking bang here in Abbottabad Cantt. I hope its not the start of something nasty :-S
1.09 a.m. 2 May

@ReallyVirtual Sohaib Athar
@m0hcin the few people online at this time of the night are saying one of the copters was not Pakistani...
1.48 a.m. 2 May

INTRO

POLITICS &
CURRENT AFFAIRS

ROYALTY &
RELIGION

CELEBRITY

SCIENCE &
NATURE

SPORT &
LEISURE

ARTS, CULTURE
& MEDIA

A TWEET A DAY

GLOSSARY
& THANKS

@ReallyVirtual Sohaib Athar
Report from a taxi driver: The army has cordoned off the crash area and is conducting door-to-door search in the surrounding
8.02 a.m. 2 May

@ReallyVirtual Sohaib Athar
RT @ISuckBigTime: Osama Bin Laden killed in Abbottabad, Pakistan.: ISI has confirmed it << Uh oh, there goes the neighborhood :-/
8.31 a.m. 2 May

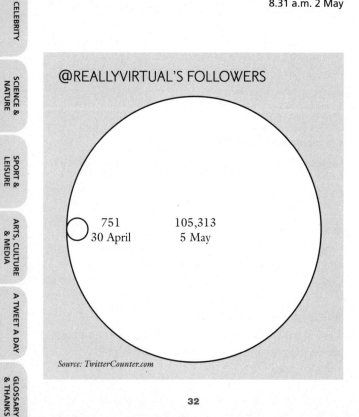

@REALLYVIRTUAL'S FOLLOWERS

751   105,313
30 April   5 May

Source: TwitterCounter.com

INTRO

POLITICS &
CURRENT AFFAIRS

ROYALTY &
RELIGION

CELEBRITY

SCIENCE &
NATURE

SPORT &
LEISURE

ARTS, CULTURE
& MEDIA

A TWEET A DAY

GLOSSARY
& THANKS

— The Tweet That Broke the News —

Keith Urbahn, chief of staff to the former Defence Secretary Donald Rumsfeld, was the first person to reveal Osama Bin Laden's death in the mainstream media. President Obama himself confirmed it at 11.35 p.m. (Eastern time).

@keithurbahn Keith Urbahn
So I'm told by a reputable person they have killed Osama Bin Laden. Hot damn.
10.25 p.m. 1 May

___ How the World Tweeted ___
Osama Bin Laden's Death

Egypt: strongly anti-US; sympathy for Osama
France: criticism of the long war that led to his death
Indonesia: distrust; scepticism; some sympathy
Pakistan: distrust; some jokes
UK: mostly critical; often humorous
USA: jokes; sharing facts; celebratory

Source: Research.ly

3,440
Average TPS over nearly two hours on the night of 1 May – the highest sustained rate to date

Source: Twitter

INTRO

POLITICS &
CURRENT AFFAIRS

ROYALTY &
RELIGION

CELEBRITY

SCIENCE &
NATURE

SPORT &
LEISURE

ARTS, CULTURE
& MEDIA

A TWEET A DAY

GLOSSARY
& THANKS

75,000

Number of times Giggs's name was
tweeted before he was named
in Parliament

*Source: Speech by Liberal
Democrat MP John Hemming
to Parliament, 23 May 2011*

— 8 MAY 2011 —

TWITTER BREAKS THE
SUPERINJUNCTIONS

Rumours of which high-profile figures had protected their
privacy with a so-called superinjunction reached wildfire
status when people began tweeting the names. On 23
May MP John Hemming revealed Welsh footballer Ryan
Giggs as one of the figures involved: Giggs had taken out
a gagging order to prevent reporting of his extra-marital
relationship with reality TV star and former Miss Wales,
Imogen Thomas.

Note: All times local to UK

@Jemima_Khan Jemima Khan
OMG- Rumour that I have a super injunction preventing
publication of "intimate" photos of me and Jeremy
Clarkson. NOT TRUE!
7.54 p.m. 8 May

@funnyhumour funny humour

Ryan Giggs is suing twitter. I can't Imogen why

12.31 a.m. 21 May

@VicHoon Vic Houghton

Ryan Giggs really doesn't understand Twitter, does he?

6.07 p.m. 21 May

@usarsnl Keith Hickey

Ryan Giggs. Imogen Thomas. Affair. Stick your super-injunction up your ass.

7.53 p.m. 21 May

@wallaceme Mark Wallace

Unsurprised Ryan Giggs has no sense of perspective - he's a man who's been praised since the age of 6 for having feet.

9.10 p.m. 21 May

@JRobertsF1 James Roberts

Ryan Giggs. Am I allowed to write that?

5.33 p.m. 23 May

@RealRobMugabe Robert Mugabe

Breaking news: on visit to Westminster Abbey, President Obama identifies the unknown soldier as Ryan Giggs.

3.24 p.m. 24 May

INTRO

POLITICS &
CURRENT AFFAIRS

ROYALTY &
RELIGION

CELEBRITY

SCIENCE &
NATURE

SPORT &
LEISURE

ARTS, CULTURE
& MEDIA

A TWEET A DAY

GLOSSARY
& THANKS

— 27 MAY 2011 —

ANTHONY WEINER
POSTS LEWD PICTURE

It was intended as a DM for a 21-year-old female follower, but instead, the married New York Democratic congress-man accidentally posted a picture of his bulging crotch to his public Twitter feed, @RepWeiner. After initially claim-ing his account had been hacked, he ultimately admitted to sending it, and resigned on 16 June.

Note: All times local to New York, NY

@BorowitzReport Andy Borowitz
BREAKING: Bill Clinton Blasts Weiner: "In my day, we'd show it to 'em in person."
10.10 p.m. 3 Jun

@jasonmustian Jason Mustian
Remember when the only people who saw a politician's penis were hookers and interns?
5.03 p.m. 6 Jun

@GeorgeTakei George Takei
If your name is "Weiner" and you hold public office, don't tempt fate with internet pics. #AreYouListeningBoehner?
10.15 a.m. 7 Jun

@theeMikeV Mike V
No joke. O'Reilly defends CBS's lack of #weiner coverage saying it isn't hard news. #weinerjokes
4.41 a.m. 11 Jun

— Death by Twitter —

When hackers took over Fox News's Twitter account @foxnewspolitics on 4 July 2011, they went big, tweeting that President Obama had been shot and killed at a restaurant in Iowa. The hashtag #obamadead soon started trending.

He wasn't alone: Jim Carrey, Justin Bieber, Christian Slater, Hugh Hefner, Jackie Chan and Charlie Sheen also saw Twitter flooded with rumours of their premature deaths in 2011.

— 4 JULY 2011 —

THE NEWS CORP HACKING SCANDAL

It wasn't the first accusation of voicemail hacking against News Corp-owned British Sunday newspaper the *News of the World*, but it was the most shocking: in the months before missing schoolgirl Milly Dowler's body was found in 2002, a private investigator hired by the paper allegedly listened to her mobile phone voicemail and deleted messages to make room for more, thereby raising false hopes that she might still be alive. Nine years on, Dowler's family discovered the truth and, in the wake of those revelations, came resignations and arrests; inquiries into police, press and political corruption; the abandonment of News Corp's plan to take over TV operator BSkyB; and one infamous shaving-foam pie.

Note: All times local to UK

INTRO

POLITICS &
CURRENT AFFAIRS

ROYALTY &
RELIGION

CELEBRITY

SCIENCE &
NATURE

SPORT &
LEISURE

ARTS, CULTURE
& MEDIA

A TWEET A DAY

GLOSSARY
& THANKS

— Who's Who —

RUPERT MURDOCH: CEO of media empire News Corp, which includes Fox, the Dow Jones, the *Wall Street Journal* and, in the UK, *The Times* and the *Sun*

JAMES MURDOCH: chairman and CEO, News Corp International; son of Rupert

REBEKAH BROOKS: editor of the *News of the World* 2000–03; chief executive of News International, the UK division of News Corp, from 2009

ANDY COULSON: editor of *News of the World* 2003–07 (resigned after one of his staff was jailed for hacking); then communications director to Conservative party leader David Cameron, who later became Prime Minister of the UK, resigned in early 2011

COLIN MYLER: last editor of the *News of the World*

NICK DAVIES: lead reporter at the *Guardian* newspaper, who uncovered the scandal

ED MILIBAND: leader of the Labour party

TOM WATSON: Labour MP who played a key role in pursuing the investigation; questioned Brooks and the Murdochs on behalf of Parliament

CHRIS BRYANT: Labour MP who also pursued the investigation

INTRO

POLITICS &
CURRENT AFFAIRS

ROYALTY &
RELIGION

CELEBRITY

SCIENCE &
NATURE

SPORT &
LEISURE

ARTS, CULTURE
& MEDIA

A TWEET A DAY

GLOSSARY
& THANKS

@GuidoFawkes Guido Fawkes
Milly hacking happened on Rebekah's watch at the
NotW, she is so **cked. That is **cked, not hacked.
5.15 p.m. 4 Jul

@Ed_Miliband Ed Miliband
Shocked by the news of the hacking of Milly Dowler's
phone. Police enquiry must find out who was
responsible.
11.11 p.m. 4 Jul

@Peston Robert Peston
*News Int passed emails to police that
seem to show Andy Coulson as editor of
NOTW authorised payments to police.
No comment from Coulson.*
10.16 p.m. 5 Jul

@paulmmace paul mace
Virgin, Tesco, Wickes, Ford, Co-Op, Sainsbury's, T-Mob,
Halifax, First Choice, TUI, Mitsibishi & Vauxhall have
pulled all #notw advertising.
4.21 p.m. 6 Jul

@robbierowantree Robbie Rowantree
Can these people stoop any lower. NoTW investigators
hacked dead soldiers families mobiles. #Notw
10.45 p.m. 6 Jul

@fieldproducer Neal Mann
Currently News International are investigating
themselves,the Met Police are investigating themselves &
the PCC are investigating themselves
8.35 a.m. 7 Jul

INTRO

POLITICS &
CURRENT AFFAIRS

ROYALTY &
RELIGION

CELEBRITY

SCIENCE &
NATURE

SPORT &
LEISURE

ARTS, CULTURE
& MEDIA

A TWEET A DAY

GLOSSARY
& THANKS

@TimGatt Tim Gatt
BREAK Sky #NOTW source: "there is mass anger in news
room. All directed at Rebekah. Colin Myler absolutely
furious. Staff devastated."
4.14 p.m. 7 Jul

@kirstymalcolm kirsty malcolm
#phonehacking #notw *NEWS OF THE WORLD
IS CLOSING ! MURDOCH
ANNOUNCES FINAL EDITION !!*
4.40 p.m. 7 Jul

@kamalahmed1 Kamal Ahmed
All in the planning - sunonsunday.co.uk and
sunonsunday.com registered two days ago #notw
5.45 p.m. 7 Jul

@martinbrunt martin brunt
Andy Coulson arrested by two teams of detectives
running separate inquiries into phone hacking and
corruption of police
11.21 a.m. 8 Jul

@MichaelWolffNYC Michael Wolff
This week will be about Rebekah Brooks trying to hold
on. She won't make it. My guess: Wednesday she goes.
12.05 p.m. 11 Jul

@caitlinmoran Caitlin Moran
So, basically, every story that's happened in the last
twelve years, the people involved were hacked. That's
what it looks like.
4.17 p.m. 11 Jul

INTRO

POLITICS &
CURRENT AFFAIRS

ROYALTY &
RELIGION

CELEBRITY

SCIENCE &
NATURE

SPORT &
LEISURE

ARTS, CULTURE
& MEDIA

A TWEET A DAY

GLOSSARY
& THANKS

@jonnelledge Jonn Elledge
You know the bit in Star Wars when the ewoks all start dancing? That's basically how I imagine the Guardian offices look right now.
2.27 p.m. 13 Jul

@johnprescott John Prescott
So BSkyB bid over. PCC to be abolished. Senior News International staff arrested. Inquiry into police and press on its way. Yep. I'm happy
2.37 p.m. 13 Jul

@LisaHendrix Lisa Hendrix
We can hope. RT @has_bookpushers Looks like Mudoch's fucked in the US. Per BBC, Sen Rockefeller is investigating 9/11 hacking allegations
5.01 p.m. 13 Jul

@ChrisBryantMP Chris Bryant
Guardian reporting official summons being delivered by serjeant at arms to james and rupert Murdoch.
They have to agree or else face commons
12.04 p.m. 14 Jul

53%

Percentage of news links that related to the hacking scandal, 4–8 July; bigger than any topic in the previous 10 months

Source: Pew Research Center's Project for Excellence in Journalism

INTRO

POLITICS &
CURRENT AFFAIRS

ROYALTY &
RELIGION

CELEBRITY

SCIENCE &
NATURE

SPORT &
LEISURE

ARTS, CULTURE
& MEDIA

A TWEET A DAY

GLOSSARY
& THANKS

@MichaelWolffNYC Michael Wolff
Rupert in WSJ: just "Minor mistakes." Rupert only gives interview to his own news outlets. Controlled reality. Closed loop.
9.57 p.m. 14 Jul

@edyong209 Ed Yong
Rebekah Brooks has resigned!
Sky bid dropped! NotW extinct!
Only four horcruxes left to go and
Murdoch will be mortal again!
11.13 a.m. 15 Jul

@MarinaHyde Marina Hyde
No surprise that Saudi prince thinks Rebekah shouldn't have been running NI. Presumably he doesn't even think she should be driving a car.
11.38 a.m. 15 Jul

@arusbridger alan rusbridger
now Les Hinton, CEO of Wall Street Journal, resigns
9.15 p.m. 15 Jul

@Bynickdavies Nick Davies
We hear Rebekah Brooks is arrested.
1.37 p.m. 17 Jul

@carlmaxim Carl Maxim
Rebekah Brooks says her arrest 'came as surprise'. The police did leave a message but I guess someone must have deleted it.
4.38 p.m. 17 Jul

@afneil Andrew Neil

So #hacking claimed jobs of two CEOs, two editors, hundreds of journalists -- now boss of #MetPolice. And the carnage has only just begun

7.43 p.m. 17 Jul

@skynewsgatherer Harriet Tolputt

Met Police Commissioner Sir Paul Stephenson resigns #phonehacking

7.53 p.m. 17 Jul

@AdweekEmma Emma Bazilian

My dad on recent NOTW happenings: "Jesus, that is some Stieg Larsson shit!"

12.02 p.m. 18 Jul

@bola_adeyemi76 Debola

John yates resigns over hackgate. Another one bites the dust. Who is next and where will it end

2.14 p.m. 18 Jul

@TelegraphNews Daily Telegraph News

Breaking: Sean Hoare, former #notw showbiz reporter&1st to allege that Andy Coulson was aware of phone #hacking found dead at his home

6.24 p.m. 18 Jul

@penjenny Jenny P

Watching Murdoch evidence to parliamentary committee. Can't believe Rupert M's "Today is the most humble day of my life". Pass the bucket.

2.46 a.m. 19 Jul

INTRO

POLITICS & CURRENT AFFAIRS

ROYALTY & RELIGION

CELEBRITY

SCIENCE & NATURE

SPORT & LEISURE

ARTS, CULTURE & MEDIA

A TWEET A DAY

GLOSSARY & THANKS

INTRO

POLITICS &
CURRENT AFFAIRS

ROYALTY &
RELIGION

CELEBRITY

SCIENCE &
NATURE

SPORT &
LEISURE

ARTS, CULTURE
& MEDIA

A TWEET A DAY

GLOSSARY
& THANKS

@bola_adeyemi76 Debola
Tom watson is really earning his pay check. This is how to
do it. Well done to him. RM is really shaking not stirred
3.04 p.m. 19 Jul

@KathViner Katharine Viner
Mensch: ;have you considered resigning?' Rupert M: 'no,
it's for others to pay. I'm the best person to clear this up'
5.24 p.m. 19 Jul

@lukejcr Luke Charters-Reid
*BREAKING: Rupert Murdoch regrets hiring
Cameron as Prime Minister.*
7.33 p.m. 21 Jul

___ Slapstick Comes ___
to the Commons

On 19 July Jonathan May-Bowles, aka stand-up
comedian Jonnie Marbles, stole the headlines when
he leapt up from the public galleries and attacked
Rupert Murdoch with a shaving-foam pie as he gave
testimony to MPs. Moments before, he sent the
following tweet:

@JonnieMarbLes Jonnie Marbles
It is a far better thing that I do now than
I have ever done before #splat
19 Jul

44

— Wendi Deng vs the Pie —

Rupert Murdoch's wife, Wendi Deng, leapt into action when the pie was thrown, slapping it back at May-Bowles for good measure.

@jonsnowC4 Jon Snow
Werndi wasn't only awake she slapped some character who appears to have gone at Rupert with a custard puie: British farce invades US tedium
19 Jul

@Aiannucci Armando Iannucci
Let's hear it for slapstick.
19 Jul

@Piers Morgan Piers Morgan
Wendi just stole all the headlines. That idiot protestor, allowed in by MPs, has single-handedly won the day's PR for the Murdochs.
19 Jul

@missVmoss Victoria Moss
this is JUST like world cup. As soon as I went to the loo, someone scored
19 Jul

INTRO

POLITICS & CURRENT AFFAIRS

ROYALTY & RELIGION

CELEBRITY

SCIENCE & NATURE

SPORT & LEISURE

ARTS, CULTURE & MEDIA

A TWEET A DAY

GLOSSARY & THANKS

INTRO

POLITICS &
CURRENT AFFAIRS

ROYALTY &
RELIGION

CELEBRITY

SCIENCE &
NATURE

SPORT &
LEISURE

ARTS, CULTURE
& MEDIA

A TWEET A DAY

GLOSSARY
& THANKS

How Politicians Use Twitter

To prove they really listen

Missouri Democratic Senator Claire McCaskill has 58,000 followers and, unlike many of her colleagues, writes all her own tweets – but she doesn't follow a soul. Her reasoning? 'I really would not have the time to read all of their tweets and would have to zoom through hundreds to seek out those tweets that are asking for help, or expressing their opinion on an issue facing us in the Senate.' (By comparison, the most popular politician on Twitter, Barack Obama, follows 700,000 accounts.)

To concede defeat

> **@foster208** John M. Foster
> Congratulations to Raul Labrador
> on a hard-earned win, and best of luck
> as Idaho's next Congressman.
> 3 Nov

To defend themselves

After the July UK Parliamentary hearing in which she questioned Rupert and James Murdoch about the hacking scandal, Conservative MP Louise Mensch found the spotlight turned on her. Lord Alan Sugar, businessman, Labour peer and star of *The Apprentice*, took to Twitter to accuse her of having abused parliamentary privilege during the hearing. She had claimed, incorrectly, that Piers Morgan had admitted in his memoirs to hacking into celebrities' voicemails while he was a newspaper editor, but refused to repeat the allegation outside Parliament, where she was protected from prosecution. Her response: to go on the attack on another subject entirely – his views on employing pregnant women. The row raged all day. A few days later, she apologised for misquoting Morgan.

To sway a vote

On Friday 29 July the White House used President Obama's account (@barackobama) to rally support for an end to the ongoing debt crisis stand-off. They tweeted the names of every Republican representative with an account, urging followers to use the hashtag #compromise, and at the end of the day told their followers, 'Thanks for contacting your legislators, and for sticking with us amid our tweeting today. We're done now, we swear.' While the barrage of well over 100 tweets in a single day lost them 36,000 followers, White House communication director Dan Pfeiffer said that the tweets (plus emails) helped pressure Congress to act; a deal was voted through on the following Monday. *See page 54*

To get down with the people

Many politicians and celebrities have a staffer write their tweets, but some have come up with a method to prove it's really them speaking. Queensland premier Anna Bligh, for instance (@TheQldPremier), has her staff append any tweets they write with Prem_Team. Any she writes herself aren't appended, but are obviously anyway from the far more relaxed tone. Emoticons and text speak abound, and on rare occasions she's been known to engage in a slanging match with disgruntled voters.

INTRO

POLITICS & CURRENT AFFAIRS

ROYALTY & RELIGION

CELEBRITY

SCIENCE & NATURE

SPORT & LEISURE

ARTS, CULTURE & MEDIA

A TWEET A DAY

GLOSSARY & THANKS

INTRO

POLITICS &
CURRENT AFFAIRS

ROYALTY &
RELIGION

CELEBRITY

SCIENCE &
NATURE

SPORT &
LEISURE

ARTS, CULTURE
& MEDIA

A TWEET A DAY

GLOSSARY
& THANKS

— 23 JULY 2011 —

THE NORWAY ATTACKS

First came the massive car bomb in Oslo's government quarter, which killed eight people and damaged the office of the prime minister. Then, two hours later, news began trickling in of another attack, this time on the island of Utøya, where a youth camp for Norway's Labour party was under way. These often confused reports were even more horrifying: after roaming the island for an hour firing his gun, Anders Bering Breivik calmly surrendered to police and was charged with both crimes. Ultimately, 69 more deaths were recorded; 50 were aged 18 or under. Many of those hiding from Breivik on the island used social media, including Twitter, to raise the alarm for fear they would be overheard by him on their phones. Those tweets are not included here.

Note: All times local to Norway

@chaglen Christian Aglen
Unreal. An entire block has exploded! Huge explosion rocks Oslo, Norway! twitpic.com/5tzsmx
3.39 p.m. 22 Jul

@rtege Rune Thomas Ege
Uvirkelige scener utenfor regeringskvartalet. Sirener, blod, knust glass, tildekkede lik, Delta og militærpoliti.
[*Surreal scenes outside the government quarter. Sirens, blood, broken glass, covered corpses, anti-terrorist and military police.*]
4.03 p.m. 22 Jul

INTRO

POLITICS &
CURRENT AFFAIRS

ROYALTY &
RELIGION

CELEBRITY

SCIENCE &
NATURE

SPORT &
LEISURE

ARTS, CULTURE
& MEDIA

A TWEET A DAY

GLOSSARY
& THANKS

@BBCBreaking BBC Breaking News
#Oslo police confirm explosion was a bomb. Live: http://
bbc.in/o2XlDx
5.10 p.m. 22 Jul

@ketilbstensrud Ketil B. Stensrud
Norwegian PM: "There is a critical situation at Utøya, and
several ongoing operations as we speak." < I've no idea
what's happening at Utøya
6.02 p.m. 22 Jul

@jorgenbp Jørgen BP
#unconfirmed rapporter om skyting og drama på #AUFs
camp på Utøya. Herregud for en dag. #oslo
[*#unconfirmed reports of shooting and drama at #Labour
Youth League camp on Utøya. Oh my god, what a day.
#oslo*]
6.06 p.m. 22 Jul

@rtege Rune Thomas Ege
*On my way to Utøya. Police check points
along the road. Surreal atmosphere.*
#oslexpl
7.09 p.m. 22 Jul

@rtege Rune Thomas Ege
Continuous line of ambulances heading for Utøya.
At least 25-30 total. 20 something police cars, as well
as five helicopters #osloexpl
7.24 p.m. 22 Jul

INTRO

POLITICS &
CURRENT AFFAIRS

ROYALTY &
RELIGION

CELEBRITY

SCIENCE &
NATURE

SPORT &
LEISURE

ARTS, CULTURE
& MEDIA

A TWEET A DAY

GLOSSARY
& THANKS

@rtege Rune Thomas Ege
Police confirms: Suspected shooter detained at Utøya
youth camp. #osloexpl
7.30 p.m. 22 Jul

@BBCBreaking BBC Breaking News
Norway police say they believe #Oslo
bomb and youth camp shooting are
connected, according to local news
agency NTB. http://bbc.in/o2XlDx
7.51 p.m. 22 Jul

@aliesbati Ali Esbati
Är oskadd efter skottdramat på Utøya. Overkligt. Var
bara tiotals meter fr gärningsmannen vid ett tilfälle. Han
var utklädd till polis/vakt.
[I'm unhurt after shooting incident on Utøya. Surreal.
Was only tens of metres from the perpetrator at one
point. He was dressed as a policeman/guard.]
8.17 p.m. 22 Jul

As in the Japanese earthquake a few months earlier,
a hashtag, #utøyasavn, soon emerged that was used
to search for missing people both on the island and
at the bomb site. As one tweeter put it, it made for
heartbreaking reading.

@aliesbati Ali Esbati
Omöjligt säga hur många som skadats eller ev dödats.
Var kaos, alla var utspridda.Har personligen sett två
orörliga på håll + flera skjutna.
[*Impossible to say how many people have been injured or
possibly killed. Was chaos, everyone was scattered. Have
personally seen two immobile on hold + many shot.*]
8.19 p.m. 22 Jul

@ketilbstensrud Ketil B. Stensrud
Disturbing scenes in Norwegian broadcast television now,
as chopper films several youths swimming for their lives
in the sea.
8.23 p.m. 22 Jul

@ketilbstensrud Ketil B. Stensrud
For the record, I feel absolutely sick. Can't believe what's
happening in my beloved country. It's time to stick
together. Forever.
8.28 p.m. 22 Jul

@rtege Rune Thomas Ege
Ambulances on docks close to lake surrounding Utøya.
Paramedics still working to save lives/treat injured in
front of our eyes #osloexpl
9.09 p.m. 22 Jul

@TonjeVassbotn Tonje Vassbotn
NRK: Survivor says gunmen dressed up
as police and lured the youths out of the
bushes so they could shoot them.
#Utoya, bit.ly/q56gl4
9.33 p.m. 22 Jul

INTRO

POLITICS &
CURRENT AFFAIRS

ROYALTY &
RELIGION

CELEBRITY

SCIENCE &
NATURE

SPORT &
LEISURE

ARTS, CULTURE
& MEDIA

A TWEET A DAY

GLOSSARY
& THANKS

@hhartz Henrik Hartz

If you're in #Oslo and a registered donor, the
blood bank needs blood type O. Call +4722118900
#osloexpl #fb #in

9.34 p.m. 22 Jul

—— Good and Bad of Twitter ——

In the aftermath of the Oslo bombing and massacre,
#Blamethemuslims was trending, despite the fact that
it was quickly apparent that a non-Muslim Norwegian was responsible. Some Twitter users, however,
decided to subvert the trend, as in this offering:

> **@1nf1d3lC4str0** Infidel Castro
> I #blamethemuslims for advances in
> science, mathematics, medicine &
> chemistry. And for developing these 100's
> of years before #Christianity.
> 24 Jul

—— 29 JULY 2011 ——
THE US DEBT CRISIS

With a deadline of 2 August before the United States'
finances would go into default, Barack Obama pressured
Republican congressmen to raise the country's debt ceiling. They wanted cuts. A compromise deal was struck on
31 July and signed into law two days later.

Note: All times local to Washington DC

INTRO

POLITICS &
CURRENT AFFAIRS

ROYALTY &
RELIGION

CELEBRITY

SCIENCE &
NATURE

SPORT &
LEISURE

ARTS, CULTURE
& MEDIA

A TWEET A DAY

GLOSSARY
& THANKS

Tweeting to Raise the Ceiling

@markos Markos Moulitsas
When are people going to stop pretending that Boehner is in charge of the House?
12.53 p.m. 28 Jul

@BarackObama Barack Obama
The time for putting party first is over. If you want to see a bipartisan #compromise, let Congress know. Call. Email. Tweet. —BO
11.45 a.m. 29 Jul

@MaddowBlog Maddow Blog
House Republicans holding out for cuts in Pell Grants -- too many poor kids going to college?
http://bit.ly/rplVo6
7.49 p.m. 29 Jul

@thinkprogress ThinkProgress
This group of Republicans is enough to make a progressive think back wistfully on George W. Bush. He was a lot more reasonable.
9.19 p.m. 30 Jul

@JPBarlow John Perry Barlow
Oh, come on, Liberals. Obama had no choice but to negotiate with these terrorists. They *want* to pull the trigger.
6.41 p.m. July 31

INTRO

POLITICS &
CURRENT AFFAIRS

ROYALTY &
RELIGION

CELEBRITY

SCIENCE &
NATURE

SPORT &
LEISURE

ARTS, CULTURE
& MEDIA

A TWEET A DAY

GLOSSARY
& THANKS

Tweeting for Cuts

@virginiafoxx Virginia Foxx
What's remarkable about the debt limit debate is that
this time it's about cutting spending, instead of 1 more
blank check for overspending.
11.38 a.m. 27 Jul

@knifework Knifework
I wouldn't care if society did collapse next week.
I've got guns, ammo, and a huge redneck family.
10.45 p.m. 28 Jul

@baseballcrank Dan McLaughlin
The President of the United States is basically doing
the same thing as a 13 year old girl trying to get
"IHeartBieber" trending.
12.30 p.m. 29 Jul

@johnboehner John Boehner
Washington Democrats are all that stand between the
American people and a responsible resolution to this
debt crisis
6.31 p.m. 29 Jul

1st

Position of #deal on US trending
topics list, 1 August

Source: Twitter

INTRO

POLITICS &
CURRENT AFFAIRS

ROYALTY &
RELIGION

CELEBRITY

SCIENCE &
NATURE

SPORT &
LEISURE

ARTS, CULTURE
& MEDIA

A TWEET A DAY

GLOSSARY
& THANKS

— 8 AUGUST 2011 —

THE LONDON RIOTS

It began with a peaceful demonstration on Saturday 6 August about the police shooting of Mark Duggan, a 29-year-old man from Tottenham, north London. That night, violence, looting and arson spilt across the neighbourhood. On Sunday night, the chaos spread to Enfield, a few miles north, and to Brixton in south London. On Monday night it was even worse, with high streets across the city and elsewhere in the UK taken over by crowds of rioters, hundreds strong, massively outnumbering the police and fire service. Two brothers and a third man died in a hit-and-run incident in Birmingham, a man died after being found shot in a car, and another died after being beaten by rioters when he was trying to put out a fire. By Tuesday night, London was quiet again, but trouble still flared in Manchester. Well over a thousand arrests were made; many more than that lost their homes or livelihoods. Initial reports that the riots had been organised on Twitter were largely dismissed, and instead attention turned to the private BlackBerry Messenger service.

Note: All times local to UK

@mslulurose Lulu Rose
The Youth of the Middle East rise up for basic freedoms. The Youth of London rise up for a HD ready 42″ Plasma TV #londonriots
7.24 a.m. 8 Aug

INTRO

POLITICS &
CURRENT AFFAIRS

ROYALTY &
RELIGION

CELEBRITY

SCIENCE &
NATURE

SPORT &
LEISURE

ARTS, CULTURE
& MEDIA

A TWEET A DAY

GLOSSARY
& THANKS

@skymarkwhite Mark White
IPCC confirm the ballistic results from bullets fired in
Mark Duggan shooting should be released in next 24hrs
#tottenahmriot
1.31 p.m. 8 Aug

@eleanormorgan eleanormorgan
Sirens so loud past my Hackney window the cat just
literally screamed.
3.51 p.m. 8 Aug

@DuwayneBrooks Duwayne Brooks
If I see anyone looting in #lewisham and I know you I'm
bringing the police to your door. I don't care who you
think you are.
3.56 p.m. 8 Aug

@eleanormorgan eleanormorgan
Just saw a gang of about 10 youths on bikes cycle past
my window, balaclavas up to their eyes.
4.58 p.m. 8 Aug

@martinbrunt martin brunt
Sources: Firearms officers involved in Mark Duggan
shooting have never claimed they were fired on.
5.53 p.m. 8 Aug

@flaneur Matthew Ogle
*My Twitter is 50% Londoners sharing
street-by-street riot info and 50%
Americans commenting on stock market
doom. PLEASE SEND CAT PICTURES*
7.30 p.m. 8 Aug

@PaulLewis Paul Lewis
It is 7.50pm and already I would say #Hackney violence worse now than last night in north London http://yfrog.com/h0keddxj
7.51 p.m. 8 Aug

@Josiensor Josie Ensor
Just got chased by a gang throwing rocks by Bethnal Green overground. they're looking for a fight.
8.10 p.m. 8 Aug

@Whatleydude James Whatley
Guardian reporter @paullewis on the BBC: "This isn't Facebook & Twitter, this is BBM. Blackberry Messaging. A closed network." #londonriots
8.15 p.m. 8 Aug

@eleanormorgan eleanormorgan
Can't actually believe what I'm seeing. Barely conscious p/man under my window. 30 or so horses just charged past.
8.36 p.m. 8 Aug

@HeardinLondon HeardinLondon
Elderly shop keeper covering his doorway in wet towels, crying. #Hackney #LondonRiots
8.37 p.m. 8 Aug

@PaulLewis Paul Lewis
#Hackney Youth: "I wanted to see us do this to the fucking Feds for years."
8.41 p.m. 8 Aug

INTRO

POLITICS & CURRENT AFFAIRS

ROYALTY & RELIGION

CELEBRITY

SCIENCE & NATURE

SPORT & LEISURE

ARTS, CULTURE & MEDIA

A TWEET A DAY

GLOSSARY & THANKS

INTRO

POLITICS &
CURRENT AFFAIRS

ROYALTY &
RELIGION

CELEBRITY

SCIENCE &
NATURE

SPORT &
LEISURE

ARTS, CULTURE
& MEDIA

A TWEET A DAY

GLOSSARY
& THANKS

@PaulLewis Paul Lewis

Police officer isolated, tripped. Mobbed with bricks and sticks. Colleagues rescued him in about ten seconds. #Hackney

8.42 p.m. 8 Aug

@quantick David Quantick

#londonriots Well, I'd say it's a cautious thumbs up for the Big Society.

8.58 p.m. 8 Aug

@SamAtRedmag sam baker

poor local shopkeepers who've worked their whole lives & are now watching it go up in smoke. No-one will help them rebuild #londonriots

9.09 p.m. 8 Aug

@fieldproducer Neal Mann

Telegraph reporting that David Cameron is coming home overnight tonight #londonriots

9.11 p.m. 8 Aug

@MartinSLewis Martin Lewis

For small traders losing liveliehood in recession many r likely on the edge anyway, no way back. Burnt shutters down for years #londonriots

9.12 p.m. 8 Aug

@janeGRAZIA JaneGRAZIA

We've got a police chief begging parents to call their kids home. Isn't it years too late for that?

9.27 p.m. 8 Aug

@Divine_Miss_Em Emily Dean
This is simply awesome PR for the Olympics..
9.27 p.m. 8 Aug

@LeighHolmwood Leigh Holmwood
CNN reporter being attacked live on air. This is
MADNESS! #londonriots
9.30 p.m. 8 Aug

@Number10gov UK Prime Minister
David Cameron to chair a COBR meeting tomorrow
morning to discuss the #Londonriots
9.41 p.m. 8 Aug

@mattcooke_uk Matt Cooke
Clapham Junction being attacked. BBC reporter say
10/11yr olds carrying goods out of shops. 'Debenhams
ransacked.' #LondonRiots
9.46 p.m. 8 Aug

@rorysmith_tel Rory Smith
Not quite sure why Sky are surprised
Waterstones isn't being looted.
"What did you get?" "Telly. You?"
"Eat, Pray, Love".
10.58 p.m. 8 Aug

@ratbanjos Nat Saunders
Gonna try sleep, golf club by my bedside. Any looter that
breaks in will have to contend with me, nude, crying,
offering them my golf club.
1.26 a.m. 9 Aug

INTRO

POLITICS &
CURRENT AFFAIRS

ROYALTY &
RELIGION

CELEBRITY

SCIENCE &
NATURE

SPORT &
LEISURE

ARTS, CULTURE
& MEDIA

A TWEET A DAY

GLOSSARY
& THANKS

@oliverthring Oliver Thring
Exactly. RT @directedbychris Norway loses 92 children &
suggests more democracy. We lose JD Sports and Nandos
& demand army & rubber bullets
1.36 a.m. 9 Aug

—— Politicians under Fire ——

Many tweeters turned their anger on the politicians:
in particular, the prime minister, David Cameron,
who was on holiday.

@Salliestweets Sally F
In April 2010 Nick Clegg warned that Tory
cuts would lead to riots. Now he's a Tory Minister
himself he sees no connection. #londonriots
8 Aug

@davidwearing David Wearing
For those of you who don't remember the 80s, this
is what Tory Britain looks like #LondonRiots
8 Aug

@indiaknight India Knight
He's completely fucked it up. He's two days late
and he's going to have a Tuscan tan.
8 Aug

@willsh john v willshire
Cameron has been monitoring the situation on an
'hourly basis'. Once after tennis, once after sauna,
once after massage... #londonriots
8 Aug

INTRO

POLITICS &
CURRENT AFFAIRS

ROYALTY &
RELIGION

CELEBRITY

SCIENCE &
NATURE

SPORT &
LEISURE

ARTS, CULTURE
& MEDIA

A TWEET A DAY

GLOSSARY
& THANKS

—— Social Media to the Rescue ——

Outraged at the devastation, plans organically grew on Twitter and Facebook to help individuals and businesses hurt by the riots.

#SOMETHINGNICEFORASHRAF: A YouTube video of bleeding Malaysian student Asyraf Haziq being mugged by people pretending to help him prompted a campaign titled 'Let's Do Something Nice for Ashraf' [*sic*]. Over £22,000 was raised, half of which he gave away to other victims.

#KEEPAARONCUTTING: Similarly, a group of interns at an advertising agency took up the story of Aaron Biber, an 89-year-old barber who thought he would have to shut down his business after his shop was looted. Their campaign raised £35,000 in three days; he said it was too much, and pledged to give away much of it.

#RIOTCLEANUP: On the morning of 9 August this hashtag was trending around the world. At the same time, an account of the same name was set up by musician Sam Duckworth, and people began organising to meet in the most damaged areas, describing volunteers as 'Wombles', after the British children's TV show about creatures that tidy up Wimbledon Common. By midday, @riotcleanup had 57,000 followers, and the streets were mostly clean.

INTRO

POLITICS &
CURRENT AFFAIRS

ROYALTY &
RELIGION

CELEBRITY

SCIENCE &
NATURE

SPORT &
LEISURE

ARTS, CULTURE
& MEDIA

A TWEET A DAY

GLOSSARY
& THANKS

@arthurascii arthurascii
Last night we needed batman. This morning we need The Wombles. #londonriots #riotcleanup
9 Aug

@MrBlakeway Scott Blakeway
Not wanting to put a dampener on the admirable @Riotcleanup - but what of they do it all again tonight? #honestquestion
9 Aug

@Riotcleanup Riot Clean Up
If they do it again. We do this again tomorrow. Solidarity for our communities. Show them they cannot win
9 Aug

@wesstreeting Wes Streeting
Last night I was angry and ashamed of violence in our city. This morning, #riotcleanup makes me proud to be a Londoner.
9 Aug

@Riotcleanup Riot Clean Up
Remember: you're a womble
9 Aug

— 2 —

ROYALTY & RELIGION

@caitlinmoran Caitlin Moran
This wedding has mainly been about
Pippa Middleton's amazing arse, hasn't it?
12.27 p.m. 29 Apr

INTRO

POLITICS &
CURRENT AFFAIRS

ROYALTY &
RELIGION

CELEBRITY

SCIENCE &
NATURE

SPORT &
LEISURE

ARTS, CULTURE
& MEDIA

A TWEET A DAY

GLOSSARY
& THANKS

— Official Royal Twitter Feeds —

TWEETER	USERNAME	FOLLOWERS
Queen Rania of Jordan	@QueenRania	1,630,091
HH Sheikh Mohammed bin Rashid Al Maktoum of Dubai	@HHShkMohd	454,052
British Monarchy	@BritishMonarchy	230,440
Clarence House (representing Charles, Camilla, William, Catherine and Harry)	@ClarenceHouse	151,838
Queen Noor Al Hussein of Jordan	@QueenNoor	99,506
Sarah Ferguson	@SarahTheDuchess	27,290
Crown Prince & Crown Princess of Norway	@Kronprinsparet	21,727
Grand-Ducal Court of Luxembourg	@CourGrandDucale	310
Serbian Monarchy	@SerbianMonarchy	207

INTRO

POLITICS & CURRENT AFFAIRS

ROYALTY & RELIGION

CELEBRITY

SCIENCE & NATURE

SPORT & LEISURE

ARTS, CULTURE & MEDIA

A TWEET A DAY

GLOSSARY & THANKS

Royalty & Religion

The guests at the wedding of Prince William and Kate Middleton may have been banned from using Twitter but for those watching at home, or even with the crowds on the Mall, it was the place to be. From the dress to the vows to the quality of the first kiss, every detail was discussed, dissected and occasionally derided. The royal family themselves got in on the act, in a way: there are dozens of parody accounts speaking on their behalf, including one for a certain dead princess. Clearly, something about the establishment seems to inspire the Twittersphere, because religious institutions also attract plenty of followers – and not a small amount of irreverence.

INTRO

POLITICS &
CURRENT AFFAIRS

ROYALTY &
RELIGION

CELEBRITY

SCIENCE &
NATURE

SPORT &
LEISURE

ARTS, CULTURE
& MEDIA

A TWEET A DAY

GLOSSARY
& THANKS

PROFILE:
@QueenRania

TWITTER BIO: 'A mum and a wife with a really cool day job...'

FULL NAME: Rania Al Abdullah, Queen Consort of Jordan

BORN: 31 August 1970, Palestine

PROFESSION: Queen, campaigner; has a degree in business administration and previously worked for Apple and Citibank

BACK STORY: Royalty's answer to Angelina Jolie, Jordan's glamorous Queen Rania campaigns via Twitter for women's education, children's welfare and cross-cultural understanding between the Islamic world and the West. Married Prince Abdullah bin Al-Hussain in 1993; became queen at 29; has four children.

NUMBER OF TWITTER USERS SHE FOLLOWS: 97

AVERAGE TWEETS PER DAY: Once or twice a week, except on special occasions

AVERAGE FOLLOWERS ADDED PER DAY: 1,000

INFLUENCE SCORE: 27.9%

IMPACT SCORE: 11.3%

TWEET STYLE: Occasionally informal, usually earnest. Sometimes live-tweets her husband's speeches in both English and Arabic. Big fan of hashtags, especially when related to Jordan or Islam.

INTRO

POLITICS &
CURRENT AFFAIRS

ROYALTY &
RELIGION

CELEBRITY

SCIENCE &
NATURE

SPORT &
LEISURE

ARTS, CULTURE
& MEDIA

A TWEET A DAY

GLOSSARY
& THANKS

IN HER OWN WORDS:

"

@QueenRania Rania Al Abdullah
Closely watching developments in #Tunisia and
praying for stability and calm for its people.
15 Jan

@QueenRania Rania Al Abdullah
Best hike ever: pistachio trees, wild poppies, water
from natural spring, glimpse of oryx, breathtaking
views...
27 Apr

@QueenRania Rania Al Abdullah
All of us in the Arab world must work together to
ensure that education is not one of the casualties of
our current unrest.
30 May

"

1

Queen Rania is also the most
popular Arab on Twitter

Source:s ArabianBusiness.com

INTRO

POLITICS &
CURRENT AFFAIRS

ROYALTY &
RELIGION

CELEBRITY

SCIENCE &
NATURE

SPORT &
LEISURE

ARTS, CULTURE
& MEDIA

A TWEET A DAY

GLOSSARY
& THANKS

— Fake Royal Twitter Feeds —

TWEETER	USERNAME	FOLLOWERS
Queen Elizabeth II	@Queen_UK	432,769
	@TheFuckingQueen	26,107
	@Queenie_Uncut	676
Prince Phillip	@TheDukeofHazard	3,594
	@HRHDoE	2,739
	@PrincePhilipHRH	931
Prince Charles	@Charles_HRH	14,110
	@PrinceCharles	6,552
	@Prince_of_Wales	4,224
Princess Diana	@DianaInHeaven	47,168
Camilla, Duchess of Cornwall	@CamillaPOW	564
Prince William	@William_HRH	46,613
	@DukeWilliam1	8,500
	@HRHPrinceWilly	2,516
	@UKPrinceWilliam	1,717
Catherine, Duchess	@HRHPrincessKate	20,031
of Cambridge	@KateDuchessofC	15,479
	@HRH_Kate	2,134
	@PrincessKateFTW	7,656
Prince Harry	@princewindsor	21,259
	@Prince___Harry	18,717
	@PrinceHarryofW	4,627
	@princeharrystag	1,117
	@HarryWalesHRH	895
	@HarryWalesUncut	443
Zara Phillips	@Royal_Zara	1,262

— (Fake) Prince Harry —

Grandson of Queen Elizabeth II, son of Charles, Prince of Wales and younger brother to Prince William, Harry has served in Afghanistan but is arguably more famous for his fun-loving, mischievous side. He has many fake profiles on Twitter.

@princeharrystag Prince Harry
Fucking hell I'm pissed out of my skull. Some lucky lady is going to have to put in overtime tonight
17 Dec

@princeharrystag Prince Harry
Fuck! I've forgotten the code to unlock my phone. Can anyone from News of the World help?
26 Jan

@HarryWalesUncut Prince Harry
Do I play it cool and laid back or show her the bodypopping? One of them will work, surely
#operationpokepippa #royalwedding
29 Apr

@princeharrystag Prince Harry
Just discovered 10 voicemails & 15 texts from Wills after he went to bed asking "How do I put this thing on?"
30 Apr

INTRO

POLITICS & CURRENT AFFAIRS

ROYALTY & RELIGION

CELEBRITY

SCIENCE & NATURE

SPORT & LEISURE

ARTS, CULTURE & MEDIA

A TWEET A DAY

GLOSSARY & THANKS

INTRO

POLITICS &
CURRENT AFFAIRS

ROYALTY &
RELIGION

CELEBRITY

SCIENCE &
NATURE

SPORT &
LEISURE

ARTS, CULTURE
& MEDIA

A TWEET A DAY

GLOSSARY
& THANKS

— 29 APRIL 2011 —

THE WEDDING OF
PRINCE WILLIAM AND
CATHERINE MIDDLETON

It may not quite have reached the three billion viewers that some experts were predicting, but on Twitter the royal wedding was all anyone wanted to talk about. That, and the maid of honour's bottom.

Note: All times local to UK

@Grazia_Live Grazia_Live
royal wedding royal wedding royal wedding royal wedding royal wedding royal wedding royal wedding royal wedding royal wedding royal wedding
6.11 a.m. 29 Apr

@royalweddingcnn Royal Wedding CNN
Happy #royalwedding day! Who's awake??
7.36 a.m. 29 Apr

@NigelSarbutts Nigel Sarbutts
Love it: The Guardian has a 'Republicans click here' button on front page which makes all wedding coverage disappear.
7.56 a.m. 29 Apr

@BBCPeterHunt Peter Hunt
Kate Middleton's new title-- Her Royal Highness the Duchess of Cambridge #BBCWedding
8.00 a.m. 29 Apr

INTRO

POLITICS &
CURRENT AFFAIRS

ROYALTY &
RELIGION

CELEBRITY

SCIENCE &
NATURE

SPORT &
LEISURE

ARTS, CULTURE
& MEDIA

A TWEET A DAY

GLOSSARY
& THANKS

@simonpegg Simon Pegg
I shit you not, I just saw a naked
Prince William handcuffed to a
lamp post in East Finchley.
8.19 a.m. 29 Apr

@BBCPeterHunt Peter Hunt
Guests, some clutching top hats, others wearing them,
arriving at the Abbey's Great North Door. #BBCWedding
8.36 a.m. 29 Apr

@RoyalBiographer Ingrid Seward
Our money is on Sarah Burton for McQueen for the dress.
Rumor has it she was spotted entering The Goring in a
fur hat yesterday...
8.43 a.m. 29 Apr

@Aiannucci Armando Iannucci
Huge crowds already gathering in London for next
Thursday's referendum.
9.07 a.m. 29 Apr

@Grazia_Live Grazia_Live
Victoria Beckham's in the queue
(yes, she's queuing! is that why
she's not smiling?) Loving the midnight
blue dress/hat though. #rw2011
9.19 a.m. 29 Apr

INTRO

POLITICS &
CURRENT AFFAIRS

ROYALTY &
RELIGION

CELEBRITY

SCIENCE &
NATURE

SPORT &
LEISURE

ARTS, CULTURE
& MEDIA

A TWEET A DAY

GLOSSARY
& THANKS

@BBCPeterHunt Peter Hunt
Diana's brother Earl Spencer queuing up to enter abbey.
Will he have to show a gas bill as ID? #BBCWedding
9.30 a.m. 29 Apr

@metoffice Met Office
Latest observation from St James's Park 11.9 C so
gradually warming up. #weather
9.53 a.m. 29 Apr

5.8 million
Tweets about the Royal Wedding
in just over four days...

...peaking at

3,966
TPS on the day of the wedding

Sources: Trendrr & Twitter

@the_archbishop The Archbishop
Arrived at the Abbey early hoping to get a glimpse of the
Beckhams #royalwedding
10.05 a.m. 29 Apr

@MrsSOsbourne Sharon Osbourne
Just saw Prince William & Prince Harry arrive at
Westminster Abbey. Magnificent Men. Diana would be
so proud.
10.25 a.m. 29 Apr

@krjmanderson Martin Anderson
Melbourne Metro rail staff member watching Royal
wedding on mobile phone on Platform 1! There's no
escaping it. #royalwedding #rw2011
10.36 a.m. 29 Apr

@caitlinmoran Caitlin Moran
Ah, the familiar jaw-angle of Prince Philip muttering
"These fucking peasants" under his breath
#whatbritainisgreatat
10.42 a.m. 29 Apr

@indiaknight India Knight
Yellow Queen. Awesome.
10.42 a.m. 29 Apr

@PrincessKateFTW Kate Middleton
I'M IN THE BLOODY CAR. LET'S ROLL.
#rw2011
10.52 a.m. 29 Apr

@DianaInHeaven Princess Diana
Ha ha ha ha! She's going in a fucking CAR! I went in a
CHARIOT!!
10.53 a.m. 29 Apr

INTRO

POLITICS &
CURRENT AFFAIRS

ROYALTY &
RELIGION

CELEBRITY

SCIENCE &
NATURE

SPORT &
LEISURE

ARTS, CULTURE
& MEDIA

A TWEET A DAY

GLOSSARY
& THANKS

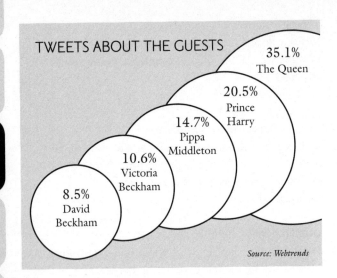

TWEETS ABOUT THE GUESTS

35.1%
The Queen

20.5%
Prince
Harry

14.7%
Pippa
Middleton

10.6%
Victoria
Beckham

8.5%
David
Beckham

Source: Webtrends

@TheSTStyle Sunday Times Style
As revealed exclusively by The Sunday Times, 6 March,
Kate Middleton wears Alexander McQueen by Sarah
Burton. Thank you. RG #rw11
11.01 a.m. 29 Apr

@TeleFashion Telegraph Fashion
Kate's train is 2.7 metres - she truly looks stunning in her
dress, made out of Chantilly lace #royalwedding
11.05 a.m. 29 Apr

@MarinaMetro Marina O'Loughlin
Carole (silently):
'squeeeeeeeeeeeeeeeeeeeeeal!!!'
11.08 a.m. 29 Apr

INTRO

POLITICS & CURRENT AFFAIRS

ROYALTY & RELIGION

CELEBRITY

SCIENCE & NATURE

SPORT & LEISURE

ARTS, CULTURE & MEDIA

A TWEET A DAY

GLOSSARY & THANKS

@ericanhk Erica NHK
William just told Kate 'You look beautiful'
11.09 a.m. 29 Apr

@antlanelondon Anthony Lane
Run, Kate/Catherine, run like the wind!
11.10 a.m. 29 Apr

@plantemily Emily Plant
aaand im crying #RW11
11.10 a.m. 29 Apr

@agirltweets agirl
NO OBEY!!!! Good girl!
11.16 a.m. 29 Apr

@fuggirls Go Fug Yourself
The Bishop's eyebrows are AWESOME. He looks like he
might moonlight at Hogwarts - J
11.20 a.m. 29 Apr

@ClarenceHouse Clarence House
The Archbishop: 'I pronounce that they be man and wife
together, in the name of the Father, and of the Son, and
of the Holy Ghost' #rw2011
11.20 a.m. 29 Apr

@nicolecav1 Nicole Cavaliere
Hey! Archbishop! You forgot 'you may now kiss the bride'
11.21 a.m. 29 Apr

@MartinSLewis Martin Lewis
Is pippa middelton's bottom trending yet?
11.21 a.m. 29 Apr

INTRO

POLITICS &
CURRENT AFFAIRS

ROYALTY &
RELIGION

CELEBRITY

SCIENCE &
NATURE

SPORT &
LEISURE

ARTS, CULTURE
& MEDIA

A TWEET A DAY

GLOSSARY
& THANKS

— Pippa Middleton's Bottom —

@MrPointyHead Daniel Maher
Can't wait for the Pippa's bum montage.
29 Apr

@caitlinmoran Caitlin Moran
This wedding has mainly been about Pippa
Middleton's amazing arse, hasn't it?
29 Apr

@SasAtRedMag Saska Graville
Pippa Middleton, a lesson in good lingerie
#royalwedding No VPL
29 Apr

@VaughanCricket Michael Vaughan
Tell you what!!! Pippa is fit...
29 Apr

@SamdeBrito Sam de Brito
WOW I JUST SAW A BLACK PERSON.
11.30 a.m. 29 Apr

@HRHPrincessKate Not Kate Middleton
Nobody told me I was going to have to sit next to nuns!
#wellscared #RoyalWedding
11.39 a.m. 29 Apr

@Queen_UK Elizabeth Windsor
Feeling slightly awkward about Princess Beatrice's hat, to
be honest.
12.02 p.m. 29 Apr

INTRO

POLITICS &
CURRENT AFFAIRS

ROYALTY &
RELIGION

CELEBRITY

SCIENCE &
NATURE

SPORT &
LEISURE

ARTS, CULTURE
& MEDIA

A TWEET A DAY

—— Beatrice's Hat ——

"

@HRHDukeOfEdin Prince Philip UNCUT
My God what the hell have the
Ferguson sprogs got on their heads?
They look like extras from the
Cantina Bar in Star Wars!
29 Apr

@fuggirls Go Fug Yourself
OH YES. EUGENIE AND BEATRICE JUST MADE MY
NIGHT. Bea's fascinator looks like a giant hand-
mirror. "Who's the nuttiest of them all..." -H
29 Apr

@UKPrinceWilliam William Windsor HRH
Poor Princess Beatrice's hat just got mauled
by the ceiling fan! Poor love she's in
floods of tears over her champagne :(
29 Apr

@EmiMarKerr Emily Williams
Princess Beatrice's hat should be turned into a child
training toilet seat. It even has the handles to carry
it around. Royal class.
29 Apr

@pourmecoffee pourmecoffee
Alright, you've had your fun. Now, PUT
AWAY THE HATS.
29 Apr

"

INTRO

POLITICS &
CURRENT AFFAIRS

ROYALTY &
RELIGION

CELEBRITY

SCIENCE &
NATURE

SPORT &
LEISURE

ARTS, CULTURE
& MEDIA

A TWEET A DAY

GLOSSARY
& THANKS

@poniewozik James Poniewozik
In a nod to tradition, networks using the original skycam
installed in roof of Westminster Abbey by Henry III in
1245. #royalwedding
12.05 p.m. 29 Apr

@HRHDukeOfEdin Prince Philip UNCUT
Well so far so good. No Asian chappies in rucksacks have
shown up though I did have my eye open for any bulges
in the Sultans sarong.
12.08 p.m. 29 Apr

@pourmecoffee pourmecoffee
*Tune in to BBC After Dark tonight for
'The Consummation.'*
12.10 p.m. 29 Apr

@diamondgeezer diamond geezer
On the Mall #dodgingthehorsepoo
1.00 p.m. 29 Apr

@BenjaminEdmonds Benjamin Edmonds
Is now #proudtobebritish as QILF is trending. Brilliant.
1.04 p.m. 29 Apr

In the USA, most tweets emanated from small towns
(such as New Haven, Connecticut, and Lubbock,
Texas) rather than big cities.
Source: Trendrr

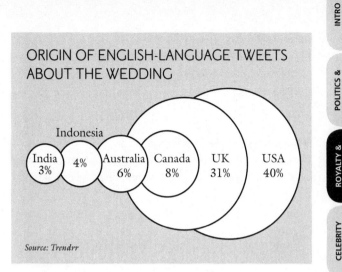

ORIGIN OF ENGLISH-LANGUAGE TWEETS ABOUT THE WEDDING

India
3%

Indonesia
4%

Australia
6%

Canada
8%

UK
31%

USA
40%

Source: Trendrr

@RoyalReporter Richard Palmer
The crowd is gradually being allowed down The Mall and will soon be let in in front of us right outside the main palace gates.
1.07 p.m. 29 Apr

@royalweddingcnn Royal Wedding CNN
They kissed! #royalwedding!
1.27 p.m. 29 Apr

@royalweddingcnn Royal Wedding CNN
The crowd is chanting 'Kiss again! Kiss again!'
#royalwedding
1.28 p.m. 29 Apr

@royalweddingcnn Royal Wedding CNN
They kissed again! #royalwedding
1.29 p.m. 29 Apr

INTRO

POLITICS & CURRENT AFFAIRS

ROYALTY & RELIGION

CELEBRITY

SCIENCE & NATURE

SPORT & LEISURE

ARTS, CULTURE & MEDIA

A TWEET A DAY

GLOSSARY & THANKS

INTRO

POLITICS &
CURRENT AFFAIRS

ROYALTY &
RELIGION

CELEBRITY

SCIENCE &
NATURE

SPORT &
LEISURE

ARTS, CULTURE
& MEDIA

A TWEET A DAY

GLOSSARY
& THANKS

@the_archbishop The Archbishop
I pray that the press didn't see Prince Harry and Pippa
Middleton in the cloisters after he took her up the aisle
#royalwedding
1.59 p.m. 29 Apr

@Queen_UK Elizabeth Windsor
Lunch finished. Queen medley coming up. Don't stop one
now, one's having such a good time, one's having a ball!
2.17 p.m. 29 Apr

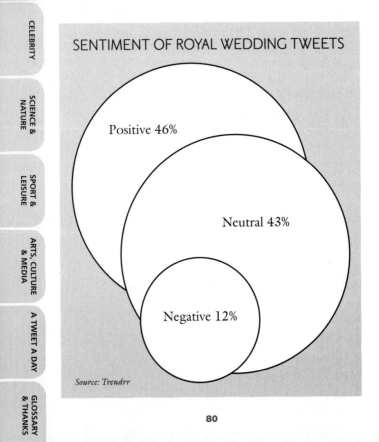

SENTIMENT OF ROYAL WEDDING TWEETS

Positive 46%

Neutral 43%

Negative 12%

Source: Trendrr

INTRO

POLITICS &
CURRENT AFFAIRS

ROYALTY &
RELIGION

CELEBRITY

SCIENCE &
NATURE

SPORT &
LEISURE

ARTS, CULTURE
& MEDIA

A TWEET A DAY

GLOSSARY
& THANKS

@hanniep Hannah
Wills driving Kate from Buckingham Palace in a 'Just
Wed' decorated Astin-Martin convertible = ADORABLE.
3.51 p.m. 29 Apr

@dgoneill Dave O'Neill
*Huge cheers on the mall as streetsweeper
goes past with bin men giving the
royal wave.* #rw2011 #onlyinlondon
8.53 p.m. 29 Apr

@andersoncooper Anderson Cooper
Of course, you can't generalize, and plenty of folks drink
in US, but I never see this much public intoxication in NY
3.20 a.m. 30 Apr

70%
said #GoRoyals

30%
said #NoRoyals

Source: @SkyNews poll

INTRO

POLITICS &
CURRENT AFFAIRS

ROYALTY &
RELIGION

CELEBRITY

SCIENCE &
NATURE

SPORT &
LEISURE

ARTS, CULTURE
& MEDIA

A TWEET A DAY

GLOSSARY
& THANKS

___ The Top Worldwide Royal ___
Wedding Trending Topics

1. William & Kate
2. #proudtobebritish
3. #royalwedding
4. #rw11
5. THEY KISSED
6. PILF
7. Buckingham Palace
8. Sarah Burton
9. QILF
10. Westminster Abbey
11. Grace Kelly
12. Pippa Middleton
13. #cnntv
14. Pippa
15. #casamentoreal
16. Abadia
17. Clarence House
18. Samantha Cameron
19. #bodareal
20. Edith Bowman

Fears that Pippa Middleton outshone her sister were proved wrong by the trending topics over the week of the wedding: she came in at numbers 12 and 14, but still higher than her supposed rival, Chelsy Davy, at 25. Numbers 15 and 19 mean 'royal wedding' in Portuguese and Spanish respectively; 16 means 'abbey' in both languages. As for 6 and 9, fill in the blanks: '_____ I'd like to fuck.'

Source: Liz Pullen, WhatTheTrend.com; stats for Saturday 23–Friday 29 April 2011

___ The Most-followed Religious ___
& Spiritual Figures

POLITICS &
CURRENT AFFAIRS

ROYALTY &
RELIGION

CELEBRITY

SCIENCE &
NATURE

SPORT &
LEISURE

ARTS, CULTURE
& MEDIA

A TWEET A DAY

GLOSSARY
& THANKS

TWEETER	USERNAME	FOLLOWERS
Rev Run	@RevRunWisdom	2,540,150
Dalai Lama	@DalaiLama	2,255,979
MC Hammer	@MCHammer	2,192,373
Rev Chris Oyakhilome	@PastorChrisLive	1,037,597
Deepak Chopra	@DeepakChopra	601,712
Rick Warren	@RickWarren	404,286
Joyce Meyer	@JoyceMeyer	369,483
Joel Osteen	@JoelOsteen	317,030
Mark Driscoll	@PastorMark	161,990
T. D. Jakes	@BishopJakes	159,366
Eckhart Tolle	@EckhartTolle	78,960
Donald Miller	@donmilleris	76,276
Jamal Bryant	@jamalhbryant	54,733
Ed Young	@EdYoung	53,756
Bill Hybels	@BillHybels	35,684
Erwin McManus	@erwinmcmanus	33,490
Joshua Harris	@HarrisJosh	32,910
Thich Nhat Hanh	@thichnhathanh	31,600
Mark Batterson	@MarkBatterson	30,857

INTRO

POLITICS &
CURRENT AFFAIRS

ROYALTY &
RELIGION

CELEBRITY

SCIENCE &
NATURE

SPORT &
LEISURE

ARTS, CULTURE
& MEDIA

A TWEET A DAY

GLOSSARY
& THANKS

PROFILE:
@RevRunWisdom

TWITTER BIO: 'Words of wisdom non-stop.. Pls don't be offended if I don't reply or follow u, But I Love you!'

FULL NAME: Joseph Ward Simmons

BORN: 14 November 1964, Queens, New York

PROFESSION: Musician, minister, self-help author and reality TV star

BACK STORY: Founder member of rap group Run-DMC, famed for the 1980s hits 'Walk This Way' and 'It's Like That'. Later became an ordained Pentecostal minister and co-wrote a parenting advice book with his wife, Justine. He has three children from a previous marriage, and a further four with Justine, one of whom died as a newborn.

NUMBER OF TWITTER USERS HE FOLLOWS: 0

AVERAGE TWEETS PER DAY: 11

AVERAGE FOLLOWERS ADDED PER DAY: 3,700

IMPACT SCORE: 92.6%

INFLUENCE SCORE: 76.9%

TWEET STYLE: Inspirational nuggets of wisdom about daily life, sometimes but not always infused with overt Christianity.

INTRO

POLITICS &
CURRENT AFFAIRS

ROYALTY &
RELIGION

CELEBRITY

SCIENCE &
NATURE

SPORT &
LEISURE

ARTS, CULTURE
& MEDIA

A TWEET A DAY

GLOSSARY
& THANKS

PROFILE:
@DalaiLama

TWITTER BIO: 'Welcome to the official Twitter page of the Office of His Holiness the 14th Dalai Lama'

FULL NAME: Jetsun Jamphel Ngawang Lobsang Yeshe Tenzin Gyatso

BORN: 6 July 1935 in Taktser, in the western Chinese province of Qinghai (or in Amdo, Tibet, depending on your political perspective)

PROFESSION: Spiritual leader of Tibetan Buddhism

BACK STORY: Born to a farming family, he was named Dalai Lama at age two. Assumed political role in 1950 after China's invasion of Tibet the previous year, and campaigns for Tibetan independence to this day. Joined Twitter in February 2010.

NUMBER OF TWITTER USERS HE FOLLOWS: 0

AVERAGE TWEETS PER DAY: 1

AVERAGE FOLLOWERS ADDED PER DAY: 4,800

IMPACT SCORE: 76.7%

INFLUENCE SCORE: 56.5%

TWEET STYLE: Philosophising mixed in with formal announcements from his staff about interviews and appearances. Reflecting his high profile in mainstream circles and not just Buddhism, he tweets about values that cross religious boundaries, such as the importance of compassion and peace.

INTRO

POLITICS &
CURRENT AFFAIRS

ROYALTY &
RELIGION

CELEBRITY

SCIENCE &
NATURE

SPORT &
LEISURE

ARTS, CULTURE
& MEDIA

A TWEET A DAY

GLOSSARY
& THANKS

IN HIS OWN WORDS:

"

@DalaiLama Dalai Lama
Being motivated by compassion and love,
respecting the rights of others – this is the real
practice of religion.
28 Jun

@DalaiLama Dalai Lama
Meet hostility and suspicion with kindness. Helping
others out of love is always the
best option.
29 Jul

"

PROFILE:
@MCHammer

TWITTER BIO: None

FULL NAME: Stanley Kirk Burrell

BORN: 30 March 1962, California

PROFESSION: Musician, dancer and preacher

BACK STORY: Found fame with his 1989 rap hit, 'U
Can't Touch This', but lost much of the fortune
that came with it. Later ordained as a preacher,
and has officiated at the weddings of celebrities
including Mötley Crüe vocalist Vince Neil. He has
five children with his wife, Stephanie, and also cares
for his nephew.

INTRO

POLITICS &
CURRENT AFFAIRS

ROYALTY &
RELIGION

CELEBRITY

SCIENCE &
NATURE

SPORT &
LEISURE

ARTS, CULTURE
& MEDIA

A TWEET A DAY

GLOSSARY
& THANKS

NUMBER OF TWITTER USERS HE FOLLOWS: 37,877

AVERAGE TWEETS PER DAY: 21

AVERAGE FOLLOWERS ADDED PER DAY: 800

IMPACT SCORE: 45.9%

INFLUENCE SCORE: 41.1%

TWEET STYLE: An early adopter of Twitter (he signed up in 2007), he is a frequent retweeter of fellow celebrities and tech news, regularly interacts with his followers, and occasionally tweets his spiritual advice.

—— Fake Religious Twitter Feeds ——

TWEETER	USERNAME	FOLLOWERS
God	@God	71,036
	@TheTweetOfGod	32,656
	@HolyGod	24,886
	@Thelordyourgod	1,544
Jesus	@Jesus	353,278
	@Jesus_Christ	9,448
Rowan Williams, Archbishop of Canterbury	@the_archbishop	325
	@NOTRDWilliams	283
Pope Benedict XVI	@thefuckingpope	7,174

INTRO

POLITICS &
CURRENT AFFAIRS

ROYALTY &
RELIGION

CELEBRITY

SCIENCE &
NATURE

SPORT &
LEISURE

ARTS, CULTURE
& MEDIA

A TWEET A DAY

GLOSSARY
& THANKS

— God Tweets —

Religious institutions may finally be catching on to the uses of social media, but not quite fast enough – all the good usernames have already been taken.

@God God
Joseph still hasn't forgiven me for referring to Mary as "my baby momma" during Mother's Day.
12 May

@TheTweetOfGod God
Though I do not answer thy tweets, know that I read them all, and that their kind words make Me wish I did not have to eventually kill thee.
14 Jul

@thelordyourgod the lord your god
THAT SADNESS YOU FEEL WHEN YOU MEET SOMEONE FROM TWITTER AND YOU FEEL COMPLETELY LET DOWN? THAT'S THE LORD YOUR GOD, ALL THE TIME
25 Nov

@HolyGod HolyGod
Happy birthday to America. May that you soon become the theocracy that I so desire.
#Electmichelebachmann
4 Jul

— The Pope Tweets —

At the time of writing, there has been only one official tweet by Pope Benedict XVI – to launch the Vatican's news feed. The fake Pope, on the other hand, is a lot chattier.

> **@news_va_en** Vatican - news
> Dear Friends, I just launched News.va Praised be our Lord Jesus Christ! With my prayers and blessings, Benedictus XVI
> 28 Jun

> **@TheFuckingPope** Pope Benny XVI
> I have a tan from the ankles down!
> 25 May

— 21 MAY 2011 —
THE RAPTURE

Christian radio broadcaster Harold Camping achieved worldwide fame thanks to his prediction that on this date Jesus Christ would return, bringing five months of plagues and earthquakes – and ultimately the end of the world. It didn't happen. He pushed Judgement Day back to October.

Note: All times local to Kiritimati, Kiribati, the first inhabited island to see the dawn, and therefore to experience the Rapture. (It was due to start at 6 p.m. 21 May wherever you were.) All tweets have been corrected to this regardless of location.

INTRO

POLITICS &
CURRENT AFFAIRS

ROYALTY &
RELIGION

CELEBRITY

SCIENCE &
NATURE

SPORT &
LEISURE

ARTS, CULTURE
& MEDIA

A TWEET A DAY

GLOSSARY
& THANKS

@nevschulman Yaniv Schulman
End of Days this weekend! I'm following @JesusChrist
just to be safe.
11.18 a.m. 19 May

@ungraceful Confounded brunette
Carb-loading in anticipation of the
rapture. I want to have enough
energy to outrun the rest of you
assholes if there's a bus to catch.
6.16 a.m 20 May

MENTIONS OF SPECIFIC RELIGIOUS BELIEFS

Christianity:	3,677,000
Islam:	1,803,000
Judaism:	505,300
Paganism:	193,200
Atheism,:	174,900
Buddhism:	110,300
Hinduism:	76,600
Kabbalah:	23,600
Scientology:	22,200
Agnosticism:	24,800
Sikhism:	23,600
Jehovah's Witnesses:	10,900

Based on search figures, Oct 2010–Aug 2011

INTRO

POLITICS & CURRENT AFFAIRS

ROYALTY & RELIGION

CELEBRITY

SCIENCE & NATURE

SPORT & LEISURE

ARTS, CULTURE & MEDIA

A TWEET A DAY

GLOSSARY & THANKS

@RuthieGledhill Ruth Gledhill
Just been asked to do TV interview about tomorrow's #rapture. Researcher said timings will change 'if it happens.' Seriously.
3.10 a.m 21 May

@BuzzFeed BuzzFeed
Never taught my cat to play the keyboard. #raptureregrets
10.01 a.m 21 May

@db Damien Basile
Today is Friday, Friday. Tomorrow is Rapture. And death comes afterwards. I don't want this world to end.
#wewewesoexcited
11.02 a.m 21 May

@PGDougSchneider Doug Schneider
Best-ever tweet from a public agency? @ddotdc Says it won't be able to fill potholes post #rapture
11.03 a.m 21 May

@jiffywild Jeff Wild
Harold Camping (end of the world nut) rec'd 80 million in contributions. It's all going to end dude, why even bother with all the money?
1.11 p.m. 21 May

@Daniel_Boerman Daniel Boerman
I'm from New Zealand, it is 6.06pm, the world has NOT ended. No earthquakes here, all waiting for the Rapture can relax for now.
8.07 p.m. 21 May

INTRO

POLITICS & CURRENT AFFAIRS

ROYALTY & RELIGION

CELEBRITY

SCIENCE & NATURE

SPORT & LEISURE

ARTS, CULTURE & MEDIA

A TWEET A DAY

GLOSSARY & THANKS

@profbriancox Brian Cox
I think we should all pretend the #rapture is happening so that when Harold Camping gets left behind later today he'll be livid.
9.08 p.m. 21 May

@renayaye Renee Asciak
I'm alive... #awkward #rapturefail
10.21 p.m. 21 May

@danielmaier Daniel Maier
People are making Rapture jokes like there's no tomorrow.
11.57 p.m. 21 May

@darthvader Darth Vader
The best part of rapturing an entire planet is getting the resulting asteroid field named after you.
#Endoftheworldconfessions
3.53 a.m 22 May

@RaptureHelpDesk Rapture Tech Support
IN CASE OF HEAVY TRAFFIC DURING THE RAPTURE, YOU MAY BE REQUIRED TO TAKE THE STAIRWAY TO HEAVEN
4.05 a.m. 22 May

@RaptureHelpDesk Rapture Tech Support
Oh boy, someone is going to lose their job over this...
6.08 a.m. 22 May

INTRO

POLITICS & CURRENT AFFAIRS

ROYALTY & RELIGION

CELEBRITY

SCIENCE & NATURE

SPORT & LEISURE

ARTS, CULTURE & MEDIA

A TWEET A DAY

GLOSSARY & THANKS

@Bumbledot Julia Calz
#myraptureplaylist Ashlee Simpson 'Pieces of Me'
...scattered throughout the universe
6.54 a.m. 22 May

@K8TXX Kat Janes
#myraptureplaylist Heaven Can Wait - Meatloaf :D
12.22 p.m. 22 May

___ Top Rapture-related ___ Trending Topics

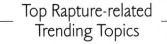

#raptureregrets   #iftheworldendsonsaturday

#endoftheworldconfessions   #myraptureplaylist

Source: Mashable

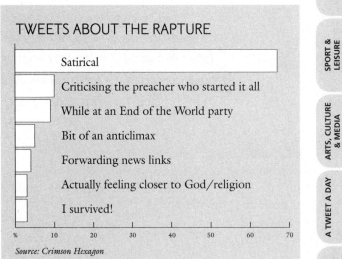

TWEETS ABOUT THE RAPTURE

Satirical

Criticising the preacher who started it all

While at an End of the World party

Bit of an anticlimax

Forwarding news links

Actually feeling closer to God/religion

I survived!

%   10   20   30   40   50   60   70

Source: Crimson Hexagon

INTRO

POLITICS &
CURRENT AFFAIRS

ROYALTY &
RELIGION

CELEBRITY

SCIENCE &
NATURE

SPORT &
LEISURE

ARTS, CULTURE
& MEDIA

A TWEET A DAY

GLOSSARY
& THANKS

20 JULY 2011

— THE CLOYNE REPORT —

In the wake of the damning Cloyne Report into sex abuse
allegations against Catholic clergy, the leader of the Irish
government, Taoiseach Enda Kenny, threatened to sever
relations between Church and State. Coming from one
of the Vatican's closest allies, this was unprecedented but,
according to Twitter, he caught the public mood.

Note: All times local to Ireland

@colmtobin Colm Tobin
BREAKING: Unconfirmed reports that Enda Kenny
has written a letter to Rupert Murdoch calling him a
"withered, power-hungry bitch".
8.32 a.m. 20 Jul

@Colmogorman Colm O'Gorman
*I cannot find the words to express
how moved I am by Taoiseachs
speech on #cloyne today. This has
been a long, hard road.*
11.48 a.m. 20 Jul

@CatholicNewsSvc Catholic News Svc
Irish PM says #Cloyne Report shows "dysfunction,
disconnection, elitism and the narcissism that dominate
the culture of the Vatican."
3.27 p.m. 20 Jul

INTRO

POLITICS &
CURRENT AFFAIRS

ROYALTY &
RELIGION

CELEBRITY

SCIENCE &
NATURE

SPORT &
LEISURE

ARTS, CULTURE
& MEDIA

A TWEET A DAY

GLOSSARY
& THANKS

@spatouttweets Dave Donnelly
Just read transcript of Enda Kenny's Dail address on the
Cloyne Report. It's what our political leaders should have
been saying for years.
3.45 p.m. 20 Jul

@cairotango Cara D
I'm still a little in shock… If he actually means what he
says, then Enda Kenny has more backbone then any
Taoiseach before him. #Cloyne
4.11 p.m. 20 Jul

@lileeny Eileen Gallagher
Enda Kenny, Ireland's Wendi Deng. Excellent speech -
now some action, please. Full speech tinyurl.com/3dwsq4f
#cloyne #endakenny
4.27 p.m. 20 Jul

@H4T Horny 4 Truth
Fair play to Enda Kenny, not afraid to call a
spade a spade or a shower of evil bastards
a shower of evil bastards #Vatican #EvilBastards
6.07 p.m. 20 Jul

@alexmassie alexmassie
The political speech of the year: http://bit.ly/r44BoU
#endakenny #cloyne #ireland
10.54 a.m. 21 Jul

@MartinFitz Martin Fitzgerald
With the Vatican scolded, & bailout rate cut, #Enda is
tonight working on Sepp Blatter to have 2010 World Cup
qualifier V France replayed.
9.48 p.m. 21 Jul

INTRO

POLITICS &
CURRENT AFFAIRS

ROYALTY &
RELIGION

CELEBRITY

SCIENCE &
NATURE

SPORT &
LEISURE

ARTS, CULTURE
& MEDIA

A TWEET A DAY

GLOSSARY
& THANKS

@philipoconnor Philip O'Connor

A message to the #Vatican- shut the door on your way out, and don't come back. You've done enough damage to the people of Ireland #Cloyne

11.13 a.m. 26 Jul

TWEETING THE SEVEN DEADLY SINS

Pride 886,000
Envy 401,000
Lust 215,000
Greed 83,400

Wrath 58,900

Sloth 51,300

Gluttony 14,500

Source: Based on search figures, Oct 2010–Aug 2011

— 3 —

CELEBRITY

@ladygaga Lady Gaga
Getting ready with my sister for the CFDA Fashion
Awards. Eyebrows burning with bleach. I should
just friggin shave them. Amen, Fashion.
4.56 p.m. 6 Jun

INTRO

POLITICS &
CURRENT AFFAIRS

ROYALTY &
RELIGION

CELEBRITY

SCIENCE &
NATURE

SPORT &
LEISURE

ARTS, CULTURE
& MEDIA

A TWEET A DAY

GLOSSARY
& THANKS

The Most-followed Celebrity Tweeters

TWEETER	USERNAME	FOLLOWERS
Lady Gaga	@ladygaga	12,948,132
Justin Bieber	@justinbieber	12,164,201
Katy Perry	@katyperry	9,389,630
Kim Kardashian	@kimkardashian	9,321,082
Britney Spears	@britneyspears	9,188,247
Shakira	@shakira	7,943,258
Taylor Swift	@taylorswift13	7,684,470
Ashton Kutcher	@aplusk	7,493,535
Ellen DeGeneres	@theellenshow	7,409,502
Oprah Winfrey	@Oprah	7,166,193
Rihanna	@rihanna	7,095,897
Selena Gomez	@selenagomez	6,988,721
Justin Timberlake	@jtimberlake	5,800,528
Eminem	@eminem	5,556,421
Nicki Minaj	@nickiminaj	5,284,052
Ryan Seacrest	@ryanseacrest	5,035,966
Ashley Tisdale	@ashleytisdale	4,970,488
Pink	@pink	4,930,515
50 Cent	@50cent	4,890,210
Mariah Carey	@mariahcarey	4,754,887

INTRO

POLITICS &
CURRENT AFFAIRS

ROYALTY &
RELIGION

CELEBRITY

SCIENCE &
NATURE

SPORT &
LEISURE

ARTS, CULTURE
& MEDIA

A TWEET A DAY

GLOSSARY
& THANKS

— Celebrity —

For the ardent fans of certain celebrities, Twitter is a competitive sport. They campaign to keep their idols in the most-followed list or the trending topics. They lap up every candid photo or detail of their everyday routine, live for a reply or even (gasp!) a follow, and they are willingly indulged by the celebrities themselves – or by whomever writes their Twitter feed for them. It's a symbiotic relationship: a flirtatious tweet from Justin Bieber can send ticket sales soaring, while Lady Gaga delights in clogging up the switchboards of her least favourite politicians. Some use it to quash rumours, and almost universally they use it to write tributes when one of their idols passes away. But not everyone is a fan, as Arnold Schwarzenegger discovered. In his case, everyone's a comedian.

INTRO

POLITICS &
CURRENT AFFAIRS

ROYALTY &
RELIGION

CELEBRITY

SCIENCE &
NATURE

SPORT &
LEISURE

ARTS, CULTURE
& MEDIA

A TWEET A DAY

GLOSSARY
& THANKS

PROFILE:
@ladygaga

TWITTER BIO: 'Mother mons†er'

FULL NAME: Stefani Joanne Angelina Germanotta

BORN: 28 March 1986, New York

PROFESSION: Singer-songwriter

BACK STORY: Famed for her outrageous fashion
sense, Lady Gaga's rise on Twitter has been as
stratospheric as her rise to fame. On 15 May she
became the first Twitter user with 10 million
followers (and gained a further 50,000 before
the day was out). A vocal supporter of gay rights
and AIDS awareness, she marshals her huge
constituency to great effect. In the run-up to the
New York State vote on gay marriage, she gave out
the contact details of state senator Mark Grisanti
during a gig and followed up with a tweet giving
out his phone number. He ultimately reversed his
position and voted in favour of the legislation,
which was approved on 24 June. The power of
Gaga? Perhaps.

NUMBER OF TWITTER USERS SHE FOLLOWS: 141,974

AVERAGE TWEETS PER DAY: 2

AVERAGE FOLLOWERS ADDED PER DAY: 24,900

IMPACT SCORE: 72.5%

INFLUENCE SCORE: 84.3%

INTERACTIVITY WITH FOLLOWERS: Intermittently tweets back to her fans (who she calls 'little monsters'), replying to questions ranging from what songs she'll be performing at gigs to her favourite type of dessert. Responded to 43 tweets on 23 May, the day her second studio album, *Born This Way*, was released.

TWEET STYLE: Affectionate, inspirational, and occasionally expresses her own fangirl side in tweets to the likes of Cher.

IN HER OWN WORDS:

> **@ladygaga** Lady Gaga
> YES Practice till u bleed! RT @maxii367 Just watched the @Mtv special on @ladygaga then practiced piano for 1 hour.#ifeelgood #lifewellspend
> 27 May

> **@ladygaga** Lady Gaga
> Getting ready with my sister for the CFDA Fashion Awards. Eyebrows burning with bleach. I should just friggin shave them. Amen, Fashion.
> 6 June

> **@ladygaga** Lady Gaga
> Omg! Latey Gaga again. I can't believe I have 12 million followers! Let's trend #12MillionMonsters! Can't wait to perform on TV twice 2nite!
> 28 Jul

INTRO

POLITICS & CURRENT AFFAIRS

ROYALTY & RELIGION

CELEBRITY

SCIENCE & NATURE

SPORT & LEISURE

ARTS, CULTURE & MEDIA

A TWEET A DAY

GLOSSARY & THANKS

INTRO

POLITICS &
CURRENT AFFAIRS

ROYALTY &
RELIGION

CELEBRITY

SCIENCE &
NATURE

SPORT &
LEISURE

ARTS, CULTURE
& MEDIA

A TWEET A DAY

GLOSSARY
& THANKS

PROFILE:
@justinbieber

TWITTER BIO: 'NEVER SAY NEVER FANCUT out
on DVD NOW!! I GOT SO MUCH LOVE FOR
THE FANS...you are always there for me and I will
always be there for you. MUCH LOVE. Thanks'

FULL NAME: Justin Drew Bieber

BORN: 1 March 1994, Ontario, Canada

PROFESSION: Singer-songwriter, actor

BACK STORY: Teen pop star with a fanbase to rival the
Beatles at their prime. In September 2010 a Twitter
employee revealed that the teen idol accounted
for 3% of all traffic on the site; the site reportedly
rejigged its algorithm to show breaking news in
the trending topics rather than consistently popular
words, partially in an attempt to prevent Bieber
clogging up the trend lists. One blip: a change to his
famous haircut diminished his power, Samson-style,
to the tune of 80,000 followers.

NUMBER OF TWITTER USERS HE FOLLOWS: 116,147

AVERAGE TWEETS PER DAY: 14

AVERAGE FOLLOWERS ADDED PER DAY: 25,100

IMPACT SCORE: 68.3%

INFLUENCE SCORE: 74.2%

INTERACTIVITY WITH FOLLOWERS: High. Frequent
retweets keep the Beliebers swooning; a follow (at

INTRO

POLITICS & CURRENT AFFAIRS

ROYALTY & RELIGION

CELEBRITY

SCIENCE & NATURE

SPORT & LEISURE

ARTS, CULTURE & MEDIA

A TWEET A DAY

GLOSSARY & THANKS

not-impossible 1:100 odds) is the ultimate reward. A tweet from Rihanna describing how he flashed his abs at her in a restaurant became the ninth most retweeted in 2010.

TWEET STYLE: Low on grammar, high on text speak and hashtags, and frequently reminiscent of a cult leader.

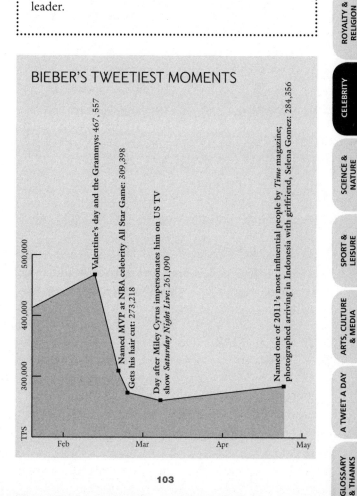

BIEBER'S TWEETIEST MOMENTS

Valentine's day and the Grammys: 467, 557

Named MVP at NBA celebrity All Star Game: 309,398
Gets his hair cut: 273,218

Day after Miley Cyrus impersonates him on US TV show *Saturday Night Live*: 261,090

Named one of 2011's most influential people by *Time* magazine; photographed arriving in Indonesia with girlfriend, Selena Gomez: 284,356

500,000
400,000
300,000
TPS

Feb · Mar · Apr · May

INTRO

POLITICS &
CURRENT AFFAIRS

ROYALTY &
RELIGION

CELEBRITY

SCIENCE &
NATURE

SPORT &
LEISURE

ARTS, CULTURE
& MEDIA

A TWEET A DAY

GLOSSARY
& THANKS

— Bieber-inspired Trending Topics —

1. Justin Bieber
2. My World 2
3. Omaha Mall
4. DIUSTIN BIBER
5. #MyOnlyQuestionIs
6. Eenie Meenie
7. bustin jieber
8. U Smile
9. Maple Syrup
10. One Less Lonely Boy

11. Wal-Mart
12. #HappyBirthdayJustin
13. Twieber
14. Jieber
15. #becauseofjustin
16. Jason McCann
17. #neversaynever
18. #5millionbeliebers
19. #justinbiebersucks
20. BUSTIN DREW JIEBER

Source: WhatTheTrend.com, collected for calendar year 2010

— How Bieber's Tweets Spark Sales —

So ardent are Bieber's Twitter followers that ticketing website Seat Geek has been able to track spikes in sales in relation to specific tweets. Even more impressive, these spikes don't come in response to plugs, but pure old-fashioned charm. Witness the effect of a pair of tweets on 30 November 2010, which proposed (to no one in partic-ular) 'a romantic candlelit dinner under the Eiffel Tower just for 2? Anyone?') and a 'random slow dance': sales promptly rose by 68%.

Source: SeatGeek.com

PROFILE:
@katyperry

TWITTER BIO: 'I kissed a girl AND diddled her skittle.'

FULL NAME: Katheryn Elizabeth Hudson

BORN: 25 October 1984, California

PROFESSION: Singer-songwriter

BACK STORY: Raised as a strict Christian, her first album consisted of gospel songs; eventually got her break with the controversial 2008 single 'I Kissed a Girl', and married shock-loving actor-comedian Russell Brand in October 2010.

NUMBER OF TWITTER USERS SHE FOLLOWS: 78

AVERAGE TWEETS PER DAY: 4

AVERAGE FOLLOWERS ADDED PER DAY: 19,100

INTERACTIVITY WITH FOLLOWERS: Intermittent. More commonly chats with famous friends, such as Rihanna and Jessie J.

IMPACT SCORE: 69.6%

INFLUENCE SCORE: 81.4%

TWEET STYLE: Often personal, she regularly mentions Brand. In July, took to Twitter to deny rumours they had split, while in March, she publicly criticised Calvin Harris, who had pulled out of her tour. Also tweets as her geek alter ego @kathybethterry.

INTRO

POLITICS &
CURRENT AFFAIRS

ROYALTY &
RELIGION

CELEBRITY

SCIENCE &
NATURE

SPORT &
LEISURE

ARTS, CULTURE
& MEDIA

A TWEET A DAY

GLOSSARY
& THANKS

IN HER OWN WORDS:

"

@katyperry Katy Perry
watching footie with the hubby, he's yelling
again & calling the tv a cocksucker. #help
28 Dec

@katyperry Katy Perry
Just cause we don't flaunt our relationship doesn't
mean there's something wrong w/it. Privacy is our
luxury. #tabloidsrtrash #gossipisgross
18 Jul

"

PROFILE:
@kimkardashian

TWITTER BIO: 'business woman, exec producer,
fashion designer, perfumista'

FULL NAME: Kimberly Noel Kardashian

BORN: 21 October 1980, California

PROFESSION: Socialite, model, reality TV star,
entrepreneur

BACK STORY: Daughter of the late lawyer Robert
Kardashian (who defended O.J. Simpson);
her mother Kris later married athlete-turned-
motivational speaker Bruce Jenner. Launched to
fame, along with two of her sisters, Khloe and

INTRO

POLITICS &
CURRENT AFFAIRS

ROYALTY &
RELIGION

CELEBRITY

SCIENCE &
NATURE

SPORT &
LEISURE

ARTS, CULTURE
& MEDIA

A TWEET A DAY

Kourtney, thanks to the reality show *Keeping up with the Kardashians*. Married Kris Humphries in August.

NUMBER OF TWITTER USERS SHE FOLLOWS: 135

AVERAGE TWEETS PER DAY: 11

AVERAGE FOLLOWERS ADDED PER DAY: 15,700

INTERACTIVITY WITH FOLLOWERS: Frequent

IMPACT SCORE: 68.5%

INFLUENCE SCORE: 79.1%

TWEET STYLE: Rarely ending a tweet without an exclamation mark, she's very affectionate towards her fans, and regularly tweets her sisters and famous friends (including Kelly Osbourne, Demi Lovato and Serena Williams). Mostly updates detail-hungry fans on her exercise regime, work schedule and social plans, incurring occasional criticism for oversharing (as in January 2011, when she posted a picture of herself in a low-cut swimsuit with the question, '#2sexy2tweet?').

IN HER OWN WORDS:

> **@KimKardashian** Kim Kardashian
> @KimKlovers omg I LOVE u! This is such a cute twitter account! I so appreciate u!
> 3 Jul

@KimKardashian Kim Kardashian
I love you more RT @KhloeKardashian: I love you @KimKardashian
5 Jul

INTRO

POLITICS &
CURRENT AFFAIRS

ROYALTY &
RELIGION

CELEBRITY

SCIENCE &
NATURE

SPORT &
LEISURE

ARTS, CULTURE
& MEDIA

A TWEET A DAY

GLOSSARY
& THANKS

@KimKardashian Kim Kardashian

I wake up & just thanks the lord for my family & friends! Seriously I love life! I love all of the people who are in my life! #LovingLife

24 Jul

PROFILE:
@britneyspears

TWITTER BIO: 'It's Britney Bitch!'

FULL NAME: Britney Jean Spears

BORN: 2 December 1981 in McComb, Mississippi; raised in Kentwood, Louisiana

PROFESSION: Singer-songwriter, actress

BACK STORY: A mother of two, Spears is as famous for her tabloid-pursued lifestyle as she is for her music. Sometimes takes to Twitter to rebutt news stories, such as one in December that alleged her boyfriend had physically abused her.

NUMBER OF TWITTER USERS SHE FOLLOWS: 419,499.

AVERAGE TWEETS PER DAY: 2

AVERAGE FOLLOWERS ADDED PER DAY IN 2011: 12,200. Lost her crown as most-followed when Lady Gaga passed her 5.6 million fans in August 2010.

IMPACT SCORE: 72.5%

INFLUENCE SCORE: 67.2%

INTRO

POLITICS &
CURRENT AFFAIRS

ROYALTY &
RELIGION

CELEBRITY

SCIENCE &
NATURE

SPORT &
LEISURE

ARTS, CULTURE
& MEDIA

A TWEET A DAY

GLOSSARY
& THANKS

INTERACTIVITY WITH FOLLOWERS: Decent. Frequent shout-outs. Follows more users than any other celebrity in the top 20 most-followed list, meaning fans have a tantalising one in 20 chance of being followed back.

TWEET STYLE: Super-enthusiastic: lots of exclamation marks and smiley faces. Often tweets her peers (including Justin Bieber, Rihanna, Christina Aguilera and 2011 tourmate Nicki Minaj).

— 10 New Arrivals on Twitter —

CELEBRITY	USERNAME	DATE OF JOINING	FOLLOWERS
Piers Morgan	@piersmorgan	16 Nov 2010	1,192,758
Charlie Sheen	@charliesheen	1 March 2011*	4,718,057
Kiefer Sutherland	@RealKiefer	1 March 2011	83,161
George Michael	@GeorgeMichael	3 March 2011	237,562
Christina Aguilera	@TheRealXtina	18 March 2011	577,007
Cheryl Cole	@cherylcole	8 March 2011	171,501
Coleen Rooney	@ColeenRoo	19 April 2011	323,378
Alec Baldwin	@AlecBaldwin	26 April 2011	277,670
Gwyneth Paltrow	@GwynethPaltrow	1 June 2011	349,409
Jerry Seinfeld	@JerrySeinfeld	15 July 2011	292,201

* *Charlie Sheen broke records by reaching 1 million followers just 25 hours and 17 minutes after creating his account.*

INTRO

POLITICS &
CURRENT AFFAIRS

ROYALTY &
RELIGION

CELEBRITY

SCIENCE &
NATURE

SPORT &
LEISURE

ARTS, CULTURE
& MEDIA

A TWEET A DAY

GLOSSARY
& THANKS

— Fake Celeb Twitter Feeds —

@pepperpaltrow Gwyneth Paltrow
Moms, what do you do when your
butler is tired of opening gifts for you?
I love hearing everyday solutions
to life's greatest challenges.
8 May

@CherylKerl Cheryl Kerl
So faw so good wur judgin heeah in America.
Leik Ah haven seen thim ger a subteetil machine
oot yet so tha's mint #xfactorusa
24 May

@Nick_Nolte Nick Nolte's Mugshot
Bout to light a couple sparklers, stick em
in my ears, cook up a speedball and run
through the park hollerin.
5 Jul

@BettyFckinWhite Betty F*ckin' White
Kids need to floss more. I just heard a young man
say that he's got bluetooth. It's sad because he is
so young.
7 Jul

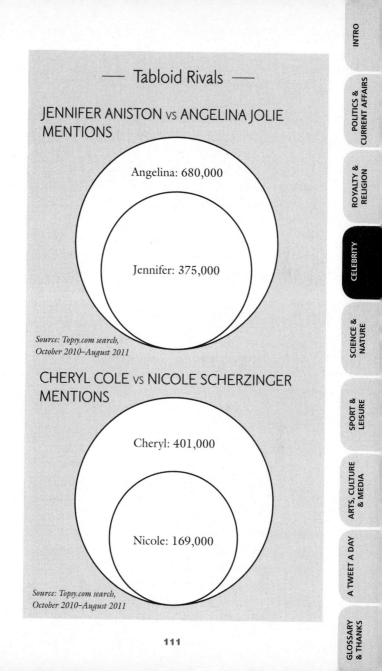

— Tabloid Rivals —

JENNIFER ANISTON vs ANGELINA JOLIE MENTIONS

Angelina: 680,000

Jennifer: 375,000

Source: Topsy.com search,
October 2010–August 2011

CHERYL COLE vs NICOLE SCHERZINGER MENTIONS

Cheryl: 401,000

Nicole: 169,000

Source: Topsy.com search,
October 2010–August 2011

INTRO

POLITICS &
CURRENT AFFAIRS

ROYALTY &
RELIGION

CELEBRITY

SCIENCE &
NATURE

SPORT &
LEISURE

ARTS, CULTURE
& MEDIA

A TWEET A DAY

GLOSSARY
& THANKS

INTRO

POLITICS &
CURRENT AFFAIRS

ROYALTY &
RELIGION

CELEBRITY

SCIENCE &
NATURE

SPORT &
LEISURE

ARTS, CULTURE
& MEDIA

A TWEET A DAY

GLOSSARY
& THANKS

—— Twibutes to Elizabeth Taylor ——

The star of countless classic films, from *National Velvet* to *Who's Afraid of Virginia Woolf*, Elizabeth Taylor died on 23 March 2011 at the Cedars-Sinai Medical Center in Los Angeles from congestive heart failure. She was 79. As in life, she was intentionally late to her own funeral.

@kingsthings Larry King
Elizabeth Taylor was a great friend, a great star and one gutsy woman. She was so special. You won't see the likes of her again...
23 Mar

@stephenfry Stephen Fry
RIP Dame Elizabeth Taylor, surely the last of a breed...
23 Mar

@SteveMartinToGo Steve Martin
I met Elizabeth Taylor several times. She was witty and self-deprecating, which I found surprising and delightful. She loved to laugh.
23 Mar

@rosannecash rosanne cash
Every year Elizabeth Taylor sent my dad a telegram (yes, telegram) for his birthday. It said: 'Remember, I'm younger than you!' (by 1 day)
23 Mar

INTRO

POLITICS &
CURRENT AFFAIRS

ROYALTY &
RELIGION

CELEBRITY

SCIENCE &
NATURE

SPORT &
LEISURE

ARTS, CULTURE
& MEDIA

A TWEET A DAY

GLOSSARY
& THANKS

___ Birth, Marriage, Flirtation ___
and Divorce

5 JUNE 2011: British couple, photographer Mary Wycherley (@marytwocats) and her husband, musician Martin Carr (@Martin_Carr) tweeted their no-holds-barred account of the birth of their daughter. It began with the waters breaking ('waters have broken like the first waters!!!!') and concluded with the baby's arrival ('It's a beautiful girl. Crying. Amazing.'). A cheer reportedly went up on a commuter train when the announcement was made.

CHRISTMAS DAY 2010: Hugh Hefner revealed his engagement to Crystal Harris with a tweet. Harris called off their June 2011 wedding a few days before the date; that news, likewise, was announced on Hefner's Twitter account.

12 DECEMBER 2010: After exchanging flirtatious tweets over several months (including one in which she said her spaniel Sammy 'sends you a special lick') and eventually being photographed kissing in public, actress and model Elizabeth Hurley and cricketer Shane Warne each confirmed via Twitter they had split from their respective spouses. In March, Hurley also used the site to deny that the couple was engaged.

5 JANUARY 2011: British glamour model Katie Price, also known as Jordan, responded to a newspaper report that her marriage was in trouble via Twitter: 'To answer my fans questions news of the world did a accurate story sunday about our marriage in crises ..always look on bright side xx.' This, apparently, was news to her husband, who tweeted (on his now-closed account) that the couple was still together; she filed for divorce two months later.

INTRO

POLITICS &
CURRENT AFFAIRS

ROYALTY &
RELIGION

CELEBRITY

SCIENCE &
NATURE

SPORT &
LEISURE

ARTS, CULTURE
& MEDIA

A TWEET A DAY

GLOSSARY
& THANKS

— 16 MAY 2011 —

SCHWARZENEGGER'S LOVE CHILD

Shortly after stepping down as Governor of California, Arnold Schwarzenegger confessed to having fathered a now 10-year-old child with a member of his household staff.

Note: All times local to California

@cpinck Chris Pinckney
Arnold said he fathered a child with a staffer? Those Austrians have the weirdest names for body parts.
3.42 a.m. 17 May

@CroweJam JD Crowe
I bet Arnold Schwarzenegger's 10 year-old love child turns out to be Danny DeVito.
9.06 a.m. 17 May

@fortunefunny Fortune Feimster
Good thing Arnold Schwarzenegger has been holding up the sanctity of marriage since apparently us gay folks don't know how to.
9.11 a.m. 17 May

@God_Damn_Batman The Batman
Arnold Schwarzenegger has an illegitimate son and a ruined marriage. But playing Mr. Freeze was still his worst decision.
12.31 p.m. 17 May

INTRO

POLITICS & CURRENT AFFAIRS

ROYALTY & RELIGION

CELEBRITY

SCIENCE & NATURE

SPORT & LEISURE

ARTS, CULTURE & MEDIA

A TWEET A DAY

GLOSSARY & THANKS

@theharryshearer Harry Shearer

Living in same house with mistress (& kid) and wife for 10 years? Arnie's a better actor than we thought. Put that guy back in movies.

8.03 a.m. 18 May

— Tweeting Without Thinking —

20 June 2011: Following the death of *Jackass* star Ryan Dunn in a high-speed car crash, American film critic Roger Ebert tweeted, 'Friends don't let jackasses drink and drive.' He later admitted his comment was 'unseemly'. His Twitter feed didn't suffer, however – that day he added nearly 8,000 followers, compared to a usual rate of around 900.

— Amy Winehouse Found Dead —

After struggling with drug and alcohol problems for many years, the singer was found dead at her north London home on 23 July 2011. She was 27. Although initially the cause of death was assumed to be an overdose, tests later showed alcohol but no drugs in her system.

@iamMarkRonson Mark Ronson
She was my musical soulmate & like a sister to me. This is one of the saddest days of my life.
24 Jul

INTRO

POLITICS &
CURRENT AFFAIRS

ROYALTY &
RELIGION

CELEBRITY

SCIENCE &
NATURE

SPORT &
LEISURE

ARTS, CULTURE
& MEDIA

A TWEET A DAY

GLOSSARY
& THANKS

@rihanna Rihanna
Dear God have mercy!!! I am SICK
about this right now! #DearAmy
23 Jul

@ricky_martin Ricky Martin
I just found out. I feel pain. I feel anger. Rest
beautiful girl rest. You are free!
23 Jul

@BigBoi Big Boi of OUTKAST
Kurt Cobain, Janis Joplin, Jim Morrison, Jimi
Hendrix and now Amy Winehouse. All died aged
27. RIP to you all. #amywinehouse
23 Jul

@NickiMinaj Nicki Minaj
Please tell me Amy Winehouse didn't die.
Is this some sick joke?
23 Jul

@DitaVonTeese Dita Von Teese
Devastated. I spent extraordinary times with Amy.
She sang for me once for hours, it was the most
beautiful& touching thing. A huge loss.
23 Jul

@ladygaga Lady Gaga
Amy changed pop music forever, I remember
knowing there was hope, and feeling not alone
because of her. She lived jazz, she lived the blues.
24 Jul

INTRO

POLITICS & CURRENT AFFAIRS

ROYALTY & RELIGION

CELEBRITY

SCIENCE & NATURE

SPORT & LEISURE

ARTS, CULTURE & MEDIA

A TWEET A DAY

GLOSSARY & THANKS

___ UK Trending Topics Shortly after ___ the Death of Amy Winehouse

1. #amywinehouse
2. #27club
3. #goplankintraffic
4. Tears Dry
5. Эми Уайнхаус
6. Robert Johnson
7. Brian Jones
8. Keith Richards
9. Kurt Cobain
10. Norway

In 2011 Amy Winehouse joined a list of musicians who didn't make it past the age of 27: Kurt Cobain, Brian Jones and Robert Johnson, as well as Jimi Hendrix, Janis Joplin and Jim Morrison. Fourth on the list above is the beginning of one of her most famous songs, 'Tears Dry on Their Own'; fifth is her name in Russian. Keith Richards was discussed by fans wondering how he'd survived his own confessed drug use. The planking trend and the attacks the previous day in Norway make up the rest of the list.

Source: Twitter

— Tweetiest Couples —

Katy Perry and Russell Brand

@rustyrockets Russell Brand
I hear @katyperry rocked Manchester-
she's the new Noel Gallagher. I'll have to
watch her eyebrows don't join up.
21 Mar

@katyperry Katy Perry
I ♥ @rustyrockets... He's my dreamboat...
5 Jun

INTRO

POLITICS &
CURRENT AFFAIRS

ROYALTY &
RELIGION

CELEBRITY

SCIENCE &
NATURE

SPORT &
LEISURE

ARTS, CULTURE
& MEDIA

A TWEET A DAY

GLOSSARY
& THANKS

Kim Kardashian and Kris Humphries

@KrisHumphries Kris Humphries
I will some time, I'm just mad that I've never seen
you in action. RT @KimKardashian: @KrisHumphries
your so cute baby! will u call in?
28 Jun

— Twitpics That Caused Trouble —

OCT AND NOV 2010: In early October, Courtney Love
accidentally posts a semi-nude picture on Twitter that was
intended for her boyfriend, and takes down her account
the next day. A few weeks later she returns and posts more
pictures, again semi-nude. The account was again taken
down.

31 DEC 2010: Russell Brand tweets a picture of his wife,
Katy Perry, without make-up; within minutes, the tweet is
deleted.

28 APR 2011: Although a picture of her breastfeeding on
her blog prompted cries of TMI, Miranda Kerr wasn't
deterred, and tweeted another in an even sexier get-up.

— 4 —

SCIENCE & NATURE

@TomokoHosaka Tomoko A. Hosaka
And we're shaking again. Oy. #JPQuake
4.46 p.m. 11 Mar

INTRO

POLITICS &
CURRENT AFFAIRS

ROYALTY &
RELIGION

CELEBRITY

SCIENCE &
NATURE

SPORT &
LEISURE

ARTS, CULTURE
& MEDIA

A TWEET A DAY

GLOSSARY
& THANKS

The Most-followed Figures
in Science & Nature

TWEETER	USERNAME	FOLLOWERS
Bill Gates, chairman of Microsoft	@BillGates	3,311,708
Noah Everett, founder of TwitPic	@NoahEverett	3,148,951
Pete Cashmore, founder of Mashable	@mashable	2,454,103
Al Gore, campaigner about climate change	@algore	2,275,419
Biz Stone, co-founder of Twitter	@biz	1,760,920
Jack Dorsey, creator of Twitter	@jack	1,715,605
Steven Johnson, author and founder of Outside.in	@StevenBJohnson	1,449,015
Padmasree Warrior, CTO of Cisco Systems	@Padmasree	1,397,446
David Pogue, tech columnist, *New York Times*	@pogue	1,383,558
Evan Williams, co-founder of Twitter	@ev	1,383,174

Science
& Nature

In a natural disaster, one of the first things that can happen is that phones become useless. The networks may be instantly overloaded but, as Twitter users discovered during Japan's devastating earthquake in March 2011, the Internet often still works. Just as in Christchurch, New Zealand's disaster a few weeks earlier, tweets helped people to find help, get reliable information or even just feel less alone. It proved time and again that people can find humour in the bleakest moments and that strangers will go out of their way to help others. Twitter is also, unsurprisingly, beloved by the techiest among us, and the year's innovations and prizes prompted plenty of debate. And for one escapee from a New York institution, it also allowed for a moment of fame.

INTRO

POLITICS &
CURRENT AFFAIRS

ROYALTY &
RELIGION

CELEBRITY

SCIENCE &
NATURE

SPORT &
LEISURE

ARTS, CULTURE
& MEDIA

A TWEET A DAY

GLOSSARY
& THANKS

INTRO

POLITICS &
CURRENT AFFAIRS

ROYALTY &
RELIGION

CELEBRITY

SCIENCE &
NATURE

SPORT &
LEISURE

ARTS, CULTURE
& MEDIA

A TWEET A DAY

GLOSSARY
& THANKS

___ Graphene Wins the ___
Nobel Prize in Physics

An atom-thick sheet of carbon that conducts heat and electricity, the thinnest, strongest material on Earth may have been created using adhesive tape and a pencil, but on 5 October 2010 it won two scientists from the University of Manchester, UK, Andre Geim and Konstantin Novoselov, the highest accolade.

66

@BillKempin Bill Kempin
The winners of the Nobel Prize for physics are responsible for graphene. I thought graphene was the drawing of bar charts on buildings.
5 Oct

@mkanders Mark Anderson
"Pencil lead & sticky tape wins Nobel"//"Graphene can be made with table sugar"... what is this, cutting-edge physics or MacGyver??
17 Nov

@wkelly wkelly
Geim, first recipient of both the Ig Nobel prize and the Nobel prize. He made a frog float and discovered graphene via use of adhesive tape.
8 Dec

99

INTRO

POLITICS &
CURRENT AFFAIRS

ROYALTY &
RELIGION

CELEBRITY

SCIENCE &
NATURE

SPORT &
LEISURE

ARTS, CULTURE
& MEDIA

A TWEET A DAY

GLOSSARY
& THANKS

— 26 DECEMBER 2010 —
THE SNOWPOCALYPSE

When a blizzard hit the east coast of the USA the day after Christmas, huge areas were quickly paralysed under 20 inches of snow. The following morning Cory Booker, Mayor of Newark, New Jersey, personally went to the rescue.

Note: All times local to New Jersey

@CoryBooker Cory Booker
I'm patroling with my shovel helping dig out. Let me know if any seniors or disabled need help.
12.09 p.m. 27 Dec

@CoryBooker Cory Booker
Responding to a distress call - woman in labor.
EMS on the way but I have a feeling my team will beat them there.
1.27 p.m. 27 Dec

@CoryBooker Cory Booker
Expecting mother is in a lot of pain but OK. We are waiting on EMS. She is a courageous young woman.
1.41 p.m. 27 Dec

@CoryBooker Cory Booker
Thanks 4 asking, back killing me: Breakfast: Advil and diet coke RT @itsmywayRob Hows ur back from lifting car last night? I hope u're OK
9.13 a.m. 28 Dec

INTRO

POLITICS &
CURRENT AFFAIRS

ROYALTY &
RELIGION

CELEBRITY

SCIENCE &
NATURE

SPORT &
LEISURE

ARTS, CULTURE
& MEDIA

A TWEET A DAY

GLOSSARY
& THANKS

@CoryBooker Cory Booker
I just doug out ur car. All the best RT @MsXmasBaby:
Is there NE city volunteers 2 dig some1 out? I'm going
2 have medical procedure done
10.41 a.m. 28 Dec

@CoryBooker Cory Booker
Just doug a car out on Springfield Ave and broke the
cardinal rule: "Lift with your Knees!!" I think I left part of
my back back there
3.03 p.m. 28 Dec

@CoryBooker Cory Booker
Where is she I will go now! RT @PrincessED89: shoveled
driveway plowers came, closed us back in. My grandma is
82 yrs old, she can't get out
5.35 p.m. 28 Dec

1,090,555: followers of
@corybooker, Mayor of Newark

277,140:
population of
Newark, New Jersey

Source: Population figure from US Census Bureau

124

INTRO

POLITICS &
CURRENT AFFAIRS

ROYALTY &
RELIGION

CELEBRITY

SCIENCE &
NATURE

SPORT &
LEISURE

ARTS, CULTURE
& MEDIA

A TWEET A DAY

GLOSSARY
& THANKS

@CoryBooker Cory Booker
Amazingly, (& again thanks 2 a crew of great volunteers)
we just had 2 dig out a huge plow truck that got stuck
here on 9th St & 12 Ave
7.18 p.m. 28 Dec

— 22 FEBRUARY 2011 —

THE CHRISTCHURCH EARTHQUAKE

At a magnitude of 6.3, the Christchurch earthquake was
smaller than the 7.1 quake that shook New Zealand's
second most populated city in September 2010. But the
one that hit at 12.51 p.m. on 22 February was closer,
shallower and, with so many buildings already weakened,
far more devastating. Many people were trapped under
rubble and it would be months before the death toll was
finally confirmed at 181. An estimated 10,000 homes were
damaged beyond repair. With phone lines overloaded, the
hashtag #eqnz was quickly taken up as a way of spreading
information, offering help and finding friends or family.

Note: All times local to Christchurch, New Zealand

@kiwiskivi Sam Kivi
Huge earthquake in chch just now short but violent. Very
disturbing. Ground still rumbling. Just had another big
shok as I write
12.57 p.m. 22 Feb

INTRO

POLITICS &
CURRENT AFFAIRS

ROYALTY &
RELIGION

CELEBRITY

SCIENCE &
NATURE

SPORT &
LEISURE

ARTS, CULTURE
& MEDIA

A TWEET A DAY

GLOSSARY
& THANKS

@nzherald nzherald
Major earthquake in Christchurch. Phone and power down in some areas - reports. #eqnz
12.59 p.m. 22 Feb

@NZStuff Stuff.co.nz News
UPDATE: Quake was magnitude 6.3, 5km deep located 10km SE of Christchurch #EQNZ
1.09 p.m. 22 Feb

@TyeTyeee Tyler
There's people just crying on the streets #eqnz
1.14 p.m. 22 Feb

@xsnowwhitestew lydsness
Our house is a shambles - more damage and sewer line in street burst in 2 places
1.15 p.m. 22 Feb

@kalena kalena
Phone lines congested. If anyone knows parents of kids at Diamond Harbour school, pls let them know all are ok #eqnz
1.17 p.m. 22 Feb

@vodafoneNZ Vodafone New Zealand
Do not overload phone lines with non-emergency calls, stick to TXT and short calls if you can #EQNZ ^ME
1.26 p.m. 22 Feb

INTRO

POLITICS & CURRENT AFFAIRS

ROYALTY & RELIGION

CELEBRITY

SCIENCE & NATURE

SPORT & LEISURE

ARTS, CULTURE & MEDIA

A TWEET A DAY

GLOSSARY & THANKS

@Martin_NZ Martin Smallman
Cathedral HAS been majorly damaged. People inside. T
1.41 p.m. 22 Feb

@JoyReidTVNZ Joy Reid
Central city.building on fire. Roads covered in silt. Bricks on footpath.people wander aimlessly.surreal
2.10 p.m. 22 Feb

@xsnowwhitestew lydsness
my street closed down. powerlines down, sink holes (my dad fell through one)
2.22 p.m. 22 Feb

@ianjameshart ian james hart
two buses crushed under rubble multiple fatalities confirmed in christchurch #eqnz #chch
2.31 p.m. 22 Feb

@jaytroyy jayyyyyyyy
im so scared i just want to go home #eqnz
2.45 p.m. 22 Feb

@resudox Steve Birnbaum
Christchurch fire chief "The best thing [for people] to do is to get out of town." #eqnz
2.47 p.m. 22 Feb

@TyeTyeee Tyler
At my grandparents with Mum and my 2 little sisters. Aftershocks keep happening and we have no power. I want to make food #eqnz
2.48 p.m. 22 Feb

INTRO

POLITICS &
CURRENT AFFAIRS

ROYALTY &
RELIGION

CELEBRITY

SCIENCE &
NATURE

SPORT &
LEISURE

ARTS, CULTURE
& MEDIA

A TWEET A DAY

GLOSSARY
& THANKS

@TyeTyeee Tyler
Sitting under a table with my sisters who are very scared
#eqnz
2.59 p.m. 22 Feb

@kiwiskivi Sam Kivi
Just retraced my steps after last shock to
find collapsed parapet right where I had
been standig 1 minute earlier. Eerie
3.01 p.m. 22 Feb

@JoyReidTVNZ Joy Reid
At makeshift triage centre in latimer square. People with
injuries flooding in. Being treated even as ground still
shakes
3.07 p.m. 22 Feb

@windingroad John Hamilton-Smith
Any news of Sumner? 89yr old mother-in-law lives by
herself, no news
3.16 p.m. 22 Feb

@safeinchch Safe in Christchurch
If you are safe, or know first-hand ABSOLUTELY that a
friend or family member is safe, Tweet here & we will RT.
3.20 p.m. 22 Feb

@SnivellingPinko • — • — — —
The din from a squillion alarms sounding simultaneously
on otherwise deserted streets = 1 of the spookiest sounds
on earth #eqnz #nzquake
3.30 p.m. 22 Feb

INTRO

POLITICS & CURRENT AFFAIRS

ROYALTY & RELIGION

CELEBRITY

SCIENCE & NATURE

SPORT & LEISURE

ARTS, CULTURE & MEDIA

A TWEET A DAY

GLOSSARY & THANKS

@windingroad John Hamilton-Smith
Call made it through to Sumner finally... thanks for the RT's. She ok house trashed. #eqnz
3.47 p.m. 22 Feb

@kimmar kimmar
If ur okay in CHCH, authorities asking you go door to door, check elderly #eqnz
3.47 p.m. 22 Feb

@NZStuff Stuff.co.nz News
Mayor Bob Parker says up to 200 people trapped, rescue workers to work through night to get to them #eqnz
6.23 p.m. 22 Feb

@kalena kalena
Have now had whisky, wine and sausage sandwiches. Shock subsiding. #eqnz
7.35 p.m. 22 Feb

—— The Kindness of Strangers ——

In the aftermath of the earthquake, offers of help spread through Twitter. Some offered spare rooms and lifts to anyone who got in touch. Others went out of their way to help people contact family members.

Note: All times local to Christchurch, New Zealand

@sgourley Sean Gourley
Anyone near Opawa in Christchurch that can check on my family there. Can't get through via cellphone #eqnz
2.20 p.m. 22 Feb

INTRO

POLITICS & CURRENT AFFAIRS

ROYALTY & RELIGION

CELEBRITY

SCIENCE & NATURE

SPORT & LEISURE

ARTS, CULTURE & MEDIA

A TWEET A DAY

GLOSSARY & THANKS

@kiwiskivi Sam Kivi
@sgourley sean I'm near opawa what's address
2.31 p.m. 22 Feb

@sgourley Sean Gourley
@kiwiskivi it's an old brick house. Not sure
if it will have held up well. Dads name is John
2.35 p.m. 22 Feb

@sgourley Sean Gourley
@kiwiskivi would appreciate it v much
if you are able to check. Worried
2.41 p.m. 22 Feb

@kiwiskivi Sam Kivi
@sgourley walking down ensors now ditched van
too slow
2.42 p.m. 22 Feb

@kiwiskivi Sam Kivi
@sgourley sean john is fine outside in car hollies is
damaged another big shock just now
2.52 p.m. 22 Feb

A major rescue effort centred on the tallest building in
Christchurch, the 26-floor Hotel Grand Chancellor.
Parts of the stairwell had collapsed, and many were
trapped inside for hours. One couple had just checked
into their room when the earthquake hit. Finding
they couldn't open the door, they called their son in
India, who reached out to everyone he could think of.
New Zealander Rob Thompson, a friend of a friend,
called the over-stretched emergency services from

Auckland, then put out the word through Twitter. A retweet was seen by a TV reporter, who happened to be with exactly the people who could help.

"

@ropate Rob Thompson
111 o/loaded, friends parents currently stuck in rm 2302 of grand chancellor. Evacuation team missed em. Any1 know how to get someone #eqnz
6.02 p.m. 22 Feb

@rgoodchild rachel goodchild
RT @ropate: 111 o/loaded, friends stuck in rm 2302 of grand chancellor. Evacuation team missed em. Any1 know how to get someone #eqnz
6.11 p.m. 22 Feb

@Naly_D Naly_D
@rgoodchild @ropate I've spoken to Civil Defence and they're sending people back.
6.12 p.m. 22 Feb

@ropate Rob Thompson
@Naly_D @rgoodchild oh my god...
Thank you thank you thank you!!!
6.27 p.m. 22 Feb

@ropate Rob Thompson
"@rgoodchild: I have never loved the invention of social media more."Me too!!!
6.48 p.m. 22 Feb

"

INTRO

POLITICS & CURRENT AFFAIRS

ROYALTY & RELIGION

CELEBRITY

SCIENCE & NATURE

SPORT & LEISURE

ARTS, CULTURE & MEDIA

A TWEET A DAY

GLOSSARY & THANKS

INTRO

POLITICS &
CURRENT AFFAIRS

ROYALTY &
RELIGION

CELEBRITY

SCIENCE &
NATURE

SPORT &
LEISURE

ARTS, CULTURE
& MEDIA

A TWEET A DAY

GLOSSARY
& THANKS

— 11 MARCH 2011 —

APPLE LAUNCHES THE IPAD2

Nicknamed the iPad1.5 by some for its minimal improvements, the device nonetheless caused huge queues on its first day on sale.

Note: All times local to California

@atk97fb Alex Klingel
I am the 30th person in line for the ipad 2. Only 6 more hours of waiting left.
8.09 a.m. 11 Mar

@kierenmccarthy Kieren McCarthy
You can buy the iPad2 from 5pm in SF today. It's 9am and there's a queue of 100 people outside the Apple store [shakes head]
9.04 a.m. 11 Mar

@swhite_hud Stephen White
Excellent, queues in America to buy the iPad 2 - reports of large numbers of the people in the queue passing the time by using their iPad 1.
12.27 p.m. 11 Mar

@Lebanesejoy Farah
First man to get an iPad 2 in New York, a Frenchman who waited 17 hours. Then he's off back to France on 8pm flight http://bit.ly/fDquA1
2.54 a.m. 12 Mar

INTRO

POLITICS &
CURRENT AFFAIRS

ROYALTY &
RELIGION

CELEBRITY

SCIENCE &
NATURE

SPORT &
LEISURE

ARTS, CULTURE
& MEDIA

A TWEET A DAY

GLOSSARY
& THANKS

@lordhunt Andrew Hunt

Standing in the cold outside the 5th Ave Apple store in a really long queue. Will the iPad2 be worth it?!

7.50 p.m. 12 Mar

1.57

Tweets about iPads per iPad sold,
22 Oct to 22 Nov 2010

Source: SimplyMeasured.com

— 11 MARCH 2011 —

THE JAPANESE EARTHQUAKE AND TSUNAMI

At 2.46 p.m. a massive undersea earthquake off the east coast of Japan set off a devastating tsunami that travelled as far as six miles inland, with waves reportedly reaching over 130 feet high. Boats, cars and people were washed inland, and a state of emergency was declared when the cooling system at the Fukushima nuclear power plant failed. Officials later put the death toll at over 15,000, with 5,000 others still missing. Other estimates put the numbers much higher.

Note: All times local to Tokyo, Japan

INTRO

POLITICS &
CURRENT AFFAIRS

ROYALTY &
RELIGION

CELEBRITY

SCIENCE &
NATURE

SPORT &
LEISURE

ARTS, CULTURE
& MEDIA

A TWEET A DAY

GLOSSARY
& THANKS

@TomokoHosaka Tomoko A. Hosaka
Wow, that was the biggest earthquake I've felt in my
nine years in Japan. Very scary.
2.55 p.m. 11 Mar

@sandrajapandra Sandra Barron
*A 6-ft cabinet full of books walked a
foot. Lid broke off the rum, emptying it,
but the Glenfiddich landed intact.*
3.04 p.m. 11 Mar

@sandrajapandra Sandra Barron
For sure. RT @danielgene: glad to hear the glenfiddich is
safe. keep it close as you guard against aftershocks.
3.14 p.m. 11 Mar

@TimeOutTokyo TimeOutTokyo
Amazing that Twitter seems to be the only way of
communicating. Phones completely down.
3.22 p.m. 11 Mar

@tokyoreporter Tokyo Reporter
Miyagi getting hit by tsunami. Ferry getting tossed in
harbor.
3.30 p.m. 11 Mar

@tokyoreporter Tokyo Reporter
*Seriously, anyone on east coast
of Japan needs to head to high
ground. Extreme disaster.*
3.35 p.m. 11 Mar

INTRO

POLITICS & CURRENT AFFAIRS

ROYALTY & RELIGION

CELEBRITY

SCIENCE & NATURE

SPORT & LEISURE

ARTS, CULTURE & MEDIA

A TWEET A DAY

GLOSSARY & THANKS

@tokyoreporter Tokyo Reporter
Sendai footage shows slow rolling water devastating farms. Now fires.
4.00 p.m. 11 Mar

@tokyoreporter Tokyo Reporter
Running cars on road in path of flood. This is beyond words.
4.01 p.m. 11 Mar

@TomokoHosaka Tomoko A. Hosaka
And we're shaking again. Oy. #JPQuake
4.46 p.m. 11 Mar

@1rick Rick Martin
still a few aftershocks. old neighbor lady quite calm as if this quake shit is routine. guess it all depends where you are. glad we're here.
5.50 p.m. 11 Mar

66%
Of news links sent on 11 March 2011 related to the Japanese disaster

Source: Pew Research Center's Project for Excellence in Journalism

5,530
Peak TPS on 11 March 2011

Source: Twitter

INTRO

POLITICS &
CURRENT AFFAIRS

ROYALTY &
RELIGION

CELEBRITY

SCIENCE &
NATURE

SPORT &
LEISURE

ARTS, CULTURE
& MEDIA

A TWEET A DAY

GLOSSARY
& THANKS

@1rick Rick Martin
remarkable that tokyo takes earthquakes as well as it does. my compliments to the engineers.
5.54 p.m. 11 Mar

@ourmaninabiko OurManInAbiko
We water from the tap has slowed to a trickle, no gas, but still have lights. Have 6-pack in fridge that must be drunk if power goes out :)
7.10 p.m. 11 Mar

@jt_sloosh Shaun McK
Reporters in The Japan Times newsroom are standing while they type their stories into the system... just in case they have to evacuate!
7.40 p.m. 11 Mar

@kenmogi Ken Mogi
People lining up at convenience stores to by food, batteries. Stations crammed with people unable to return to home. #japan #earthquake
8.55 p.m. 11 Mar

@kenmogi Ken Mogi
Cabinet secretary stresses that at present there is no explicit danger of nuclear leak. #japan #earthquake
9.54 p.m. 11 Mar

@TomokoHosaka Tomoko A. Hosaka
Japanese police: 200-300 bodies have been found in a northeastern coastal area where a massive earthquake spawned tsunami. #JPQuake
10.57 p.m. 11 Mar

INTRO

POLITICS &
CURRENT AFFAIRS

ROYALTY &
RELIGION

CELEBRITY

SCIENCE &
NATURE

SPORT &
LEISURE

ARTS, CULTURE
& MEDIA

A TWEET A DAY

GLOSSARY
& THANKS

246,075

Number of tweets using the term
'earthquake' posted by end
of 11 March 2011

Source: Daily Telegraph, UK

@BlaisePlant Blaise Plant
Currently 2am, power still out, cold. Keeping positive,
but so many people have been injured, or killed. It's hard
to sleep. Unimaginable
2.04 a.m. 12 Mar

@tamegoeswild Joseph Tame
ok, time to get a few hours sleep. Wearing jeans and
warm top. Packed suitcase by door just in case. Not
looking forward to tomorrow's news
2.31 a.m. 12 Mar

@TomokoHosaka Tomoko A. Hosaka
It's 5am. Need to sleep, or I won't be functional
tomorrow. Thank you for all your kind messages, RTs and
follows. #JPQuake #earthquake
5.10 a.m. 12 Mar

@makiwi Makiko Itoh (maki)
according to Yomiuri, radiation levels 8x outside of gates,
1000x inside central control room in nuclear power plant
#japan #earthquake
7.15 a.m. 12 Mar

INTRO

POLITICS &
CURRENT AFFAIRS

ROYALTY &
RELIGION

CELEBRITY

SCIENCE &
NATURE

SPORT &
LEISURE

ARTS, CULTURE
& MEDIA

A TWEET A DAY

GLOSSARY
& THANKS

@makiwi Makiko Itoh (maki)
packaged emergency food boxes w/bottled water, rice
pack, retort food being handed out at train stations..i
dunno, that's impressive somehow
7.43 a.m. 12 Mar

@kenmogi Ken Mogi
This just in. Pressure release operation in Fukushima
Nuclear Plant halted due to high radio activity.
#earthquake #japan NHK tv.
12.14 p.m. 12 Mar

@kyotofoodie Kyoto Foodie
Finally got my friend in Sendai on the phone. No
electricity, gas or water. He didn't know the magnitude
or epicenter - no tv or internet.
12.40 p.m. 12 Mar

@kenmogi Ken Mogi
BREAKING NEWS NHK REPORTS
DETECTION OF MELTDOWN AT
FUKUSHIMA POWER PLANT #earthquake #japan
2.17 p.m. 12 Mar

@martyn_williams Martyn Williams
24 hours after massive quake, tidal wave slammed
Japan, bigger developing story is possible meltdown at
Fukushima No.1 nuclear plant
2.53 p.m. 12 Mar

@jdierkes Julian Dierkes
Several locations completely destroyed, almost all in coastal towns, suggesting that the tsunami was much worse than the #jpquake
4.55 p.m. 12 Mar

@jdierkes Julian Dierkes
Death toll above 1,000 now. >500 victims in Miyagi Pref, >200 in Iwate #jpquake
4.57 p.m. 12 Mar

@happyten Eric
Meltdown & liquefy fuel rods carries different meaning. Don't RT of unsure info. Pls RT only official info. #jisin #genpatsu
5.39 p.m. 12 Mar

@makiwi Makiko Itoh (maki)
"in the US during the hurricane ppl were charging $10 for a bottle of water. in Japan stores are giving out water 4 free." fwiw.
10.13 p.m. 12 Mar

@happyten Eric
MAny households put out signs of "Free to use toilet here." These are the initiatives of all people. Your helps are appreciated!
6.05 a.m. 13 Mar

@Matt_Alt Matt Alt
Mail just got delivered. After all of this. That's Tokyo for you.
10.28 a.m. 13 Mar

INTRO

POLITICS & CURRENT AFFAIRS

ROYALTY & RELIGION

CELEBRITY

SCIENCE & NATURE

SPORT & LEISURE

ARTS, CULTURE & MEDIA

A TWEET A DAY

GLOSSARY & THANKS

INTRO

POLITICS &
CURRENT AFFAIRS

ROYALTY &
RELIGION

CELEBRITY

SCIENCE &
NATURE

SPORT &
LEISURE

ARTS, CULTURE
& MEDIA

A TWEET A DAY

GLOSSARY
& THANKS

@BlaisePlant Blaise Plant

No more tremors...very calm now in Sendai...hope it stays like this

4.59 p.m. 13 Mar

—— Bravery in Unexpected Quarters ——

One Twitter user's father was among hundreds of retired and older workers who volunteered to help at the damaged Fukushima nuclear plant because radiation can take years to cause ill health. This post was retweeted over 20,000 times; she has since deleted her account.

父が明日、福島原発の応援に派遣されます。半年後定年を迎える父が自ら志願したと聞き、涙が出そうになりました。「今の対応次第で原発の未来が変わる。使命感を持っていく。」家では頼りなく感じる父ですが、私は今日程誇りに思ったことはありません。無事の帰宅を祈ります。#jishin

[*Tomorrow my father is heading off to the Fukushima plant. I almost burst into tears when I learned my dad, who's about to retire in six months, had volunteered to help there. 'The future of nuclear energy depends on us and I simply cannot do otherwise,' he explained. I wouldn't say that my dad has much of a presence at home but I've never felt as proud of him as I do today. We're praying for him to come home safe and sound.* #earthquake]

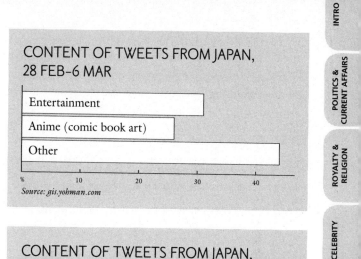

CONTENT OF TWEETS FROM JAPAN, 28 FEB–6 MAR

Entertainment

Anime (comic book art)

Other

| % | 10 | 20 | 30 | 40 |

Source: gis.yohman.com

CONTENT OF TWEETS FROM JAPAN, 11 MAR

Earthquake

Transportation

Entertainment

Other

| % | 10 | 20 | 30 | 40 | 50 | 60 | 70 |

Source: gis.yohman.com

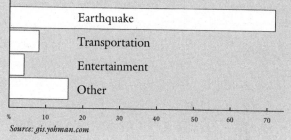

The Most Commonly Tweeted Words in Japan during March 2011

1. Earthquake
2. Area struck by disaster
3. Blackout
4. Trains
5. Scheduled blackout
6. Conserve electricity
7. Tsunami
8. Nuclear power plant
9. Taking refuge
10. Victims of disaster

Source: Tokyohive.com

INTRO

POLITICS & CURRENT AFFAIRS

ROYALTY & RELIGION

CELEBRITY

SCIENCE & NATURE

SPORT & LEISURE

ARTS, CULTURE & MEDIA

A TWEET A DAY

GLOSSARY & THANKS

INTRO

POLITICS &
CURRENT AFFAIRS

ROYALTY &
RELIGION

CELEBRITY

SCIENCE &
NATURE

SPORT &
LEISURE

ARTS, CULTURE
& MEDIA

A TWEET A DAY

GLOSSARY
& THANKS

— Hashtags Come into Their Own —

Within a few days of the earthquake, Twitter Japan announced a set of hashtags designed to help disseminate information in English and Japanese:

#JISHIN (meaning 'earthquake') for general information

#J_J_HELPME to help rescuers locate people who were trapped

#ANPI for confirmation of safety of places and individuals

#HINAN ('finding shelter') for evacuation information.

— Humour in Tragedy —

> **@jcexplorer** Daniel O'Grady
> #japan While they're at getting coolant 4 the reactor, cud they get some warmant 4 the weather? #IReallyShoulntBeComplaining
> 13 Mar

@1rick Rick Martin
There are going to be a lot of twitter users that I'm gonna want to sit down and have a beer with after this #jpquake ordeal is over.
15 Mar

> **@Matt_Alt** Matt Alt
> Now here's a precaution I can get behind. RT @beerkat Beer may work to protect human body against radiation http://bit.ly/fd1LSY
> 15 Mar

INTRO

POLITICS & CURRENT AFFAIRS

ROYALTY & RELIGION

CELEBRITY

SCIENCE & NATURE

SPORT & LEISURE

ARTS, CULTURE & MEDIA

A TWEET A DAY

GLOSSARY & THANKS

@security4all Security4all
Arrived in Tokyo, no zombies at the airport. Didn't
need that crowbar after all. Dropping plans of
today and helping out at relief center.
20 Mar

— Tweeting Without Thinking —

AMERICAN COMEDIAN AND VOICE-OVER ARTIST GILBERT GOTT-
FRIED was fired by insurance company Aflac, whose adverts
he voiced, for making a series of jokes on Twitter in the
wake of the Japanese disaster. They included this one:
'Japan is really advanced. They don't go to the beach. The
beach comes to them.' He later apologised.

THE AMERICAN MUSICIAN 50 CENT was roundly derided for
this tweet: 'Look this is very serious people I had to evacuate all my hoe's from LA,Hawaii and Japan. I had to do it.
Lol.' He seemed unfazed by his critics: 'Some of my tweets
are ignorant I do it for shock value. Hate it or love it. I'm
cool either way 50cent.'

BRITISH FILM DIRECTOR MICHAEL WINNER made an equally
thoughtless gaffe, musing that an event being planned in his
honour might suffer as a result: 'Tsunami may produce big
waves in santa monica will that affect my audience tonite.'

INTRO

POLITICS &
CURRENT AFFAIRS

ROYALTY &
RELIGION

CELEBRITY

SCIENCE &
NATURE

SPORT &
LEISURE

ARTS, CULTURE
& MEDIA

A TWEET A DAY

GLOSSARY
& THANKS

— 28 MARCH 2011 —

THE BRONX ZOO COBRA ESCAPES

When the two-foot long Egyptian cobra went missing from the New York zoo, her fictional alter ego appeared on Twitter and lost no time in going out on the town, or in gaining followers. By the time she was found (inside the reptile house) a week later, she had over 200,000 followers. Below are tweets from her first day of freedom.

Note: All times local to New York

@BronxZoosCobra Bronx Zoo's Cobra
I want to thank those animals from the movie "Madagascar." They were a real inspiration.
1.44 p.m. 28 Mar

@BronxZoosCobra Bronx Zoo's Cobra
I should take in a Broadway show. Anyone heard anything about this "Spiderman" musical?
1.50 p.m. 28 Mar

@BronxZoosCobra Bronx Zoo's Cobra
Anyone know if Rebecca Black lives in NYC? No reason.
2.20 p.m. 28 Mar

@BronxZoosCobra Bronx Zoo's Cobra
What does it take to get a cab in this city?! It's cause I'm not white isn't it.
3.21 p.m. 28 Mar

INTRO

POLITICS & CURRENT AFFAIRS

ROYALTY & RELIGION

CELEBRITY

SCIENCE & NATURE

SPORT & LEISURE

ARTS, CULTURE & MEDIA

A TWEET A DAY

GLOSSARY & THANKS

@BronxZoosCobra Bronx Zoo's Cobra

Holding very still in the snake exhibit at the Museum of Natural History. This is gonna be hilarious!

4.59 p.m. 28 Mar

@BronxZoosCobra Bronx Zoo's Cobra

Dear @CharlieSheen, know what's better than tiger's blood? Cobra venom. #winning #snakeonthetown Also I'm 20 inches long. Just sayin'.

7.14 p.m. 28 Mar

— 8 JULY 2011 —

THE SPACE SHUTTLE'S FINAL MISSION

Amidst cuts to their budgets, NASA ended the shuttle's 30 years of service. Astronauts Chris Ferguson, Doug Hurley, Sandy Magnus and Rex Walheim delivered supplies and a logistics module to the six staff of the International Space Station (including Ron Gawan and Satoshi Furukawa), landing safely back on Earth on 21 July.

Note: All times local to Washington DC

@Astro_Sandy Sandy Magnus

System briefs and weather brief complete. Scattered showers for tomorrow so who knows what will happen. Family time later today.

9.20 a.m. 7 Jul

INTRO

POLITICS &
CURRENT AFFAIRS

ROYALTY &
RELIGION

CELEBRITY

SCIENCE &
NATURE

SPORT &
LEISURE

ARTS, CULTURE
& MEDIA

A TWEET A DAY

GLOSSARY
& THANKS

@Astro_Ron Ron Garan
Just watched the launch of Atlantis live #FromSpace
onboard the #!SS God Speed #STS135! See you in a
couple of days #NASA
11.46 a.m. 8 Jul

@Astro_Ron Ron Garan
#Atlantis is Here!! I'll post a picture of the docking
tomorrow. It's my new all time favorite Shuttle px!
Stay tuned #NASA #STS135
7.11 p.m. 11 Jul

@Astro_Satoshi 古川聡（ＪＡＸＡ宇宙飛行士）
On July 13, the wakeup music for Shuttle crew was Elton
John's. The night before, Commander told us "Would
you like to come to listen ?".
12.04 a.m. 14 Jul

@Astro_Rex Rex J. Walheim
Gorgeous views backing away from ISS. Emotional
departure. Start packing for home tomorrow. Busy, tired,
smiling.
7.12 a.m. 19 Jul

@Astro_Satoshi 古川聡（ＪＡＸＡ宇宙飛行士）
The final space shuttle landed safely. Reentry is one of
the most risky moment, so I am glad to hear the news.
4.07 a.m. 22 Jul

@Astro_Rex Rex J. Walheim
Thanks for all the great welcome home messages! It
really warms my heart. I finally got some sleep. A little
sore, but very happy!!!
11.34 p.m. 22 Jul

— 5 —

SPORT & LEISURE

@Alex_Kay_DM ALEX KAY
And Murray reaches his first Wimbledon final,
destroying Nadal in four sets. Oh, wait...
7.42 p.m. 1 Jul

INTRO

POLITICS &
CURRENT AFFAIRS

ROYALTY &
RELIGION

CELEBRITY

SCIENCE &
NATURE

SPORT &
LEISURE

ARTS, CULTURE
& MEDIA

A TWEET A DAY

GLOSSARY
& THANKS

—— The Most-followed Athletes ——

TWEETER	USERNAME	FOLLOWERS
Ricardo Izecson dos Santos Leite, soccer	@KAKA	5,589,992
Shaquille O'Neal, basketball	@shaq	4,245,568
Cristiano Ronaldo, soccer	@Cristiano	3,927,325
Lance Armstrong, cycling	@lancearmstrong	3,032,048
Chad Ochocinco, American football	@ochocinco	2,649,655
Tony Hawk, skateboarding	@tonyhawk	2,604,769
LeBron James, basketball	@kingjames	2,413,550
Dwight Howard, basketball	@DwightHoward	2,226,600
Serena Williams, tennis	@serenawilliams	2,197,389
Claro Ronaldo, soccer	@ClaroRonaldo	2,191,816
Mano Menezes, soccer	@manomenezes	2,064,845
Neymar Júnior, soccer	@Njr92	2,054,660
Ryan Sheckler, skateboarder	@RyanSheckler	2,002,801
Ronaldinho Gaúcho, soccer	@10Ronaldinho	1,997,992
Reggie Bush, American football	@reggie_bush	1,910,313
Paul Pierce, basketball	@paulpierce34	1,890,757
Lamar Odom, basketball	@RealLamarOdom	1,751,510
Diego Forlan, soccer	@DiegoForlan7	1,676,741
Dwyane Wade, basketball	@DwyaneWade	1,621,747
Dana White, boxing	@danawhite	1,569,122

Sport & Leisure

Is it really any surprise that five of the top 10 tweetiest moments of the year involved sport? And it's not just about sharing the score. For professional and armchair commentators alike, Twitter is the perfect medium: it's just enough space to let you vent, gloat or offer your opinion to a much wider audience than your living room or even a pub could hold. What you might not guess, however, is precisely which game was playing on each of the occasions that a sports event broke the tweets-per-second record this year. And away from the arenas, courts and pitches, people are spending their free time tweeting top chefs with their cooking questions, and maintaining carefully updated feeds on behalf of their pets. Yes, you read that right: animals are joining Twitter in their thousands.

INTRO

POLITICS & CURRENT AFFAIRS

ROYALTY & RELIGION

CELEBRITY

SCIENCE & NATURE

SPORT & LEISURE

ARTS, CULTURE & MEDIA

A TWEET A DAY

GLOSSARY & THANKS

INTRO

POLITICS &
CURRENT AFFAIRS

ROYALTY &
RELIGION

CELEBRITY

SCIENCE &
NATURE

SPORT &
LEISURE

ARTS, CULTURE
& MEDIA

A TWEET A DAY

GLOSSARY
& THANKS

PROFILE:
@KAKA

TWITTER BIO: 'Um cristao, marido e pai. Que ama o futebol' [*A Christian, husband and father. Who loves football*]

FULL NAME: Ricardo Izecson dos Santos Leite, nicknamed Kaká

BORN: 22 April 1982, Brasília, Brazil

PROFESSION: Soccer player

BACK STORY: Began his career at São Paolo FC aged eight, going on to play for the senior team from 2001. A devout Christian whose faith was strengthened by his remarkable recovery from a broken vertebra caused by a swimming accident in 2000, he tithes a portion of his earnings to his church. Signed to AC Milan in 2003, and then to Real Madrid six years later for a world record-breaking £57 million. Married to his childhood sweetheart, Caroline Celico, he has two children. Campaigns for the United Nations World Food Program.

NUMBER OF TWITTER USERS HE FOLLOWS: 320

AVERAGE TWEETS PER DAY: 1, but replied to over 80 well-wishers on his birthday

AVERAGE FOLLOWERS ADDED PER DAY: 14,800

IMPACT SCORE: 75.8%

INFLUENCE SCORE: 37.7%

TWEET STYLE: Mainly in Portuguese, but sometimes in English. Frequently responds to his fans, and corrals their support for good causes.

IN HIS OWN WORDS:

> **@KAKA** Kaka
> Celebrating a victory and a goal, with some friends and family. I m so happy. #TksLord
> 9 Jan

@KAKA Kaka
Let's make Easter a special day feeding hungry kids. Their future is in our hands. God bless you !!
@wefeedback http://bit.ly/g3yBL8
23 Apr

PROFILE: @shaq

TWITTER BIO: 'VERY QUOTATIOUS, I PERFORM RANDOM ACTS OF SHAQNESS'

FULL NAME: Shaquille Rashaun O'Neal

BORN: 6 March 1972, Newark, New Jersey

PROFESSION: Basketball player, retired

BACK STORY: At 7 foot 1 inch, Shaq was seemingly destined for basketball. His NBA career began with the Orlando Magic team in 1992, and he played with various other teams, including the Los Angeles

151

POLITICS & CURRENT AFFAIRS

ROYALTY & RELIGION

CELEBRITY

SCIENCE & NATURE

SPORT & LEISURE

ARTS, CULTURE & MEDIA

A TWEET A DAY

GLOSSARY & THANKS

INTRO

POLITICS &
CURRENT AFFAIRS

ROYALTY &
RELIGION

CELEBRITY

SCIENCE &
NATURE

SPORT &
LEISURE

ARTS, CULTURE
& MEDIA

A TWEET A DAY

GLOSSARY
& THANKS

Lakers, becoming one of only three players to win NBA MVP (Most Valuable Player), All-Star Game MVP and Finals MVP awards in a single year. He ended his professional career at the Boston Celtics in 2011, a season that was plagued by injury, announcing his retirement on Twitter on 1 June 2011. He has also released five rap albums and trained as a reserve police officer. He is divorced with five children.

NUMBER OF TWITTER USERS HE FOLLOWS: 636

AVERAGE TWEETS PER DAY: 2

AVERAGE FOLLOWERS ADDED PER DAY: 3,800

IMPACT SCORE: 77.2%

INFLUENCE SCORE: 89.5 %

TWEET STYLE: Informal. Very self-referential, and amusing with it. Frequently posts links to video status updates at tout.com, a company in which he has an equity stake.

IN HIS OWN WORDS:

@SHAQ SHAQ

fill in da blank, my new years shaqalution is _____

22 Dec

@SHAQ SHAQ

da president wants u 2 get fit so he calld on me shaqretary of state 2 help bit.ly/PALA_SHAQ #challengeyourself

20 Jul

INTRO

POLITICS & CURRENT AFFAIRS

ROYALTY & RELIGION

CELEBRITY

SCIENCE & NATURE

SPORT & LEISURE

ARTS, CULTURE & MEDIA

A TWEET A DAY

GLOSSARY & THANKS

PROFILE:
@Cristiano

TWITTER BIO: None

FULL NAME: Cristiano Ronaldo dos Santos Aveiro

BORN: 5 February 1985, Madeira, Portugal

PROFESSION: Soccer player

BACK STORY: Signed to Manchester United at 18 and joined Real Madrid in 2009, at which point he became the highest paid footballer in the world. A prolific goal scorer, he broke his club's record last season with 51 goals. In July 2010 he became a father to Cristiano Jr, and has sole custody; he is currently dating Russian model Irina Shayk.

NUMBER OF TWITTER USERS HE FOLLOWS: 51

AVERAGE TWEETS PER DAY: 1

AVERAGE FOLLOWERS ADDED PER DAY: 11,300

IMPACT SCORE: 72.9%

INFLUENCE SCORE: 68.9%

TWEET STYLE: Uses English, Spanish and Portuguese. Mainly quite formal updates.

IN HIS OWN WORDS:

@Cristiano Cristiano Ronaldo
We are excited to win the Copa del Rey today! It's been several years, and now it's time to celebrate! http://say.ly/ATagIm

21 Apr

INTRO

POLITICS &
CURRENT AFFAIRS

ROYALTY &
RELIGION

CELEBRITY

SCIENCE &
NATURE

SPORT &
LEISURE

ARTS, CULTURE
& MEDIA

A TWEET A DAY

GLOSSARY
& THANKS

@Cristiano Cristiano Ronaldo
Portugal 1 - Norway 0. Difficult game but we got
the result. Did you watch the game?
5 Jun

— Brian Wilson's Beard —

The relief pitcher Brian Wilson's team, the San Francisco Giants, may have won this year's World Series, but his extraordinary facial hair won a decent chunk of the attention. It has several of its own Twitter accounts; @BeardOfBrian, with nearly 13,000 followers, is the biggest.

@BeardOfBrian Brian Wilson's Beard
The #SFGiants are keeping their World Series
trophy safe inside of Brian Wilson's Beard
until they arrive in San Francisco.
2 Nov

@BeardOfBrian Brian Wilson's Beard
You can lead a horse to water, but only the Beard
can make it drink.
2 Nov

@BeardOfBrian Brian Wilson's Beard
The only thing thicker than Brian Wilson's Beard
is Brian Wilson's Beard when it's wet.
4 Nov

INTRO

POLITICS &
CURRENT AFFAIRS

ROYALTY &
RELIGION

CELEBRITY

SCIENCE &
NATURE

SPORT &
LEISURE

ARTS, CULTURE
& MEDIA

A TWEET A DAY

GLOSSARY
& THANKS

— 26 DECEMBER 2010 —
THE ASHES

This year, for the biennial showdown between old rivals England and Australia, it was the latter's turn to host. As ever, Melbourne Cricket Ground was packed for the fourth of the five test series and, despite the score standing at one test all with another drawn, the home side was confident – they hadn't lost to their old enemy on their own soil since 1986.

Note: All times local to Melbourne, Australia

@abcgrandstand abcgrandstand
England captain Andrew Strauss wins the toss and opts to bat at MCG #ashes
11.06 a.m. 26 Dec

@bestbells Helen Shearan
Hussey out. COME ON ENGLAND!!! #ashes
12.23 p.m. 26 Dec

@pnoony Paul Noon
#ashes heavy rain at the MCG trying to keep warm until play starts again
1.15 p.m. 26 Dec

@the_topspin Lawrence Booth
England are loving these conditions - could be Derby on a damp Wednesday
2.28 p.m. 26 Dec

INTRO

POLITICS &
CURRENT AFFAIRS

ROYALTY &
RELIGION

CELEBRITY

SCIENCE &
NATURE

SPORT &
LEISURE

ARTS, CULTURE
& MEDIA

A TWEET A DAY

GLOSSARY
& THANKS

@TheTrout91 Chris
Aussies are crumbling! Let's hope we don't!
2.35 p.m. 26 Dec

@matt_armstrong Matt Armstrong
Lowest ever score in the first innings of a test match at
the G, apparently. Australia all out for 98... Beautiful.
#ashes #mcg
3.16 p.m. 26 Dec

@johnnyminkley Johnny Minkley
An hour's play remaining and Aussie fans are FLEEING
the MCG in their THOUSANDS. Cheerio! #ashes
5.55 p.m. 26 Dec

@Sports_k1ng Phil Ikenasio
Australian group huddle...
Punter: what do we do now...
Watson: start praying for rain lol #ashes
6.03 p.m. 26 Dec

@Aggersashes Jonathan Agnew
Last over. 98 all out plays 157 for 0. Can't believe what
I've seen here today
6.46 p.m. 26 Dec

@zhoeg Zhoe
Just woke up to hear Ashes update. You've got to be
kidding Aussies! #fb
8.31 p.m. 26 Dec

@ChrisBeanland Christopher Beanland
Replace Ponting and Hughes with Helen Daniels and
Madge Bishop? #Ashes
10.50 p.m. 26 Dec

@psam Sameer Panchangam
You all have to watch Ponting on TV right now. He's
totally lost it! Asks for a review, asks batsman, argues
with umpire. Not Out! #Ashes
1.46 p.m. 27 Dec

@Aggersashes Jonathan Agnew
Another outstanding day for England - a lead of 346 at
the end of the second day!! Ponting will surely be called
to the headmaster's study.
6.22 p.m. 27 Dec

@warne888 Shane Warne
*Morning What's everyones thoughts
what today is going to bring ? My rain
dance didn't work.. Clear blue sky and
warm and sunny ! Dam !!*
8.45 a.m. 28 Dec

@bennie_james Ben Szota
Alright, We'll Call It A Draw. #ashes
12.32 p.m. 28 Dec

@miller_cricket Andrew Miller
Massive boos for Ponting, swiftly drowned out by
raucous cheers ... I think opinion is split on the skipper
today ... #ashes
1.51 p.m. 28 Dec

INTRO

POLITICS &
CURRENT AFFAIRS

ROYALTY &
RELIGION

CELEBRITY

SCIENCE &
NATURE

SPORT &
LEISURE

ARTS, CULTURE
& MEDIA

A TWEET A DAY

GLOSSARY
& THANKS

@andre_crow Andrew Crow
OUT! Ponting has gone!
Tim Bresnan you BEAUTY! #ashes
3.15 p.m. 28 Dec

@timcoombs79 Tim Coombs
Hussey out for a duck...think we might finish this today!
#Ashes
4.06 p.m. 28 Dec

@flyingperonis flyingperonis
@aggersashes in the South stand the Aussies are taking
their lead from the batsman and leaving the MCG as
quickly as possible #ashes
4.08 p.m. 28 Dec

@warne888 Shane Warne
England on fire. And have the Aussies in all sorts of
trouble. They have played excellent cricket all series.
Probably only had 3 bad days
4.45 p.m. 28 Dec

@Pam_nAshes Pam Nash
Looks like there are only England
supporters in the stands, the MCG looks
almost empty. Aussies are
SO temperamental ;o) #ashes
10.20 a.m. 29 Dec

INTRO

POLITICS & CURRENT AFFAIRS

ROYALTY & RELIGION

CELEBRITY

SCIENCE & NATURE

SPORT & LEISURE

ARTS, CULTURE & MEDIA

A TWEET A DAY

GLOSSARY & THANKS

@maxwalterssport Max Walters
Streaming #ashes, it's Aussie commentary and they're marvelling at England's fantastic bowling! with no Harris its 2 wickets to go! Come on!
10.45 a.m. 29 Dec

@nezbleu Dr Hfuhruhurr
Have some of that Aussies!!! England retain #Ashes
11.49 a.m. Dec 29

@warne888 Shane Warne
Congrats to the England cricket team on retaining the ashes .. It has taken 24 years for England to do it in Aust.. Well done and Congrats
11.59 a.m. 29 Dec

@Prince_James Peter Johnson
oh no, some poms are starting to feel sorry for ponting instead of hating him...clearest sign yet we're fucked #ashes
12.25 p.m. 29 Dec

@William_HRH Prince William
England retain the Ashes, but unsure if it is constitutionally acceptable to celebrate given one is a future head of the Australian state?!?
9.24 p.m. 29 Dec

INTRO

POLITICS &
CURRENT AFFAIRS

ROYALTY &
RELIGION

CELEBRITY

SCIENCE &
NATURE

SPORT &
LEISURE

ARTS, CULTURE
& MEDIA

A TWEET A DAY

GLOSSARY
& THANKS

— A Case of Mistaken Identity —

When the 2010 Ashes began on 25 November, Massachusetts babysitter Ashley Kerekes unwittingly became
the target of thousands of cricket fans wanting to find
out the score. She knew nothing about cricket – the
handle @theashes is her nickname. Before long, she
had 13,500 followers, and at 11.20 p.m. tweeted her
frustration at all the questions.

Note: Time local to Massachusetts

@theashes Ashley Kerekes
**I am NOT A FREAKING CRICKET MATCH!!! That
means you** @matywilson @zandertrego
@thesummats @atonyboffey @faz1988 **and MORE**
26 Nov

Eventually, though, she saw the funny side and an
Australian airline flew her to Sydney for the fifth test.

— Tweeting without Thinking —

9 JANUARY 2011: After a match in which Manchester
United were awarded a controversial penalty and Liver-
pool's captain was sent off, the latter team's midfielder
Ryan Babel tweeted a doctored picture of the referee,
Howard Webb, wearing a Man U strip. The Football Association charged him with improper conduct – the first time
a footballer was charged over a tweet.

INTRO

POLITICS &
CURRENT AFFAIRS

ROYALTY &
RELIGION

CELEBRITY

SCIENCE &
NATURE

SPORT &
LEISURE

ARTS, CULTURE
& MEDIA

A TWEET A DAY

GLOSSARY
& THANKS

— 6 FEBRUARY 2011 —

SUPER BOWL XLV

When the Green Bay Packers faced the Pittsburgh Steelers in Dallas, the game wasn't all that sports fans were tweeting about. As ever, the half-time show and the commercials took up much of the conversation.

Note: All times local to Texas

@jasonjwilde Jason Wilde
Airfare: $600. Hotel: $2000. Ticket: $800. Not having an actual seat at SBXLV: Priceless.
4.27 p.m. 6 Feb

@AP_NFL AP_NFL
Latest on Cowboys Stadium: 400 people sent home, 850 given somewhere else to sit because temp seating wasn't ready for #SB45. –dmz
4.52 p.m. 6 Feb

@AP_NFL AP_NFL
First score of the Super Bowl: Rodgers 29-yard TD pass. #Packers lead #Steelers 7-0 with 3:44 left in 1Q -dmz
6.01 p.m. 6 Feb

@packers Green Bay Packers
The Packers have scored first in all five of their Super Bowl appearances.
6.02 p.m. 6 Feb

INTRO

POLITICS &
CURRENT AFFAIRS

ROYALTY &
RELIGION

CELEBRITY

SCIENCE &
NATURE

SPORT &
LEISURE

ARTS, CULTURE
& MEDIA

A TWEET A DAY

GLOSSARY
& THANKS

@PAIGER33 Paige Pearson
Holy mother of cheese! Collins pick 6! 14-0 #Packers
6.08 p.m. 6 Feb

3 million
Number of tweets sent by viewers
of the Super Bowl

Source: Trendrr

@Eric_Edholm Eric Edholm
Sanders threw helmet after foot injury. Sounds very bad.
#Steelers
6.29 p.m. 6 Feb

@wingoz trey wingo
And the steelers are in the danger zone. Pack gets ball to
start 2nd half...
6.43 p.m. 6 Feb

@Steelersdepot Steelers Depot
TD back in it!
6.56 p.m. 6 Feb

@chris_jenkins34 Chris Jenkins
WOW, another dropped TD by Jones.
7.40 p.m. 6 Feb

@steelers Pittsburgh Steelers
34 takes it in for 6. 21-17. Come on people. Let's hear
your support!
7.43 p.m. 6 Feb

@Steelersdepot Steelers Depot
Here we go Steelers,
Here we go!!!!!!!!!!!!! BELIEVE!
7.48 p.m. 6 Feb

@nytbishop Greg Bishop
Remember when it seemed like every Super Bowl was a blowout? Last four have been amazing games. Giants, Steelers, Saints, now this ...
8.52 p.m. 6 Feb

@AnthonyQuintano Anthony Quintano
For all you whiners in the 1st Quarter who said this game was boring. Now what? #sb45 #superbowl
8.52 p.m. 6 Feb

@packers Green Bay Packers
Rodgers takes another knee... the Packers have won Super Bowl XLV.
9.07 p.m. 6 Feb

4,064

Peak tweets per second during the Super Bowl, at 9.09 p.m.

Source: Twitter

INTRO

POLITICS &
CURRENT AFFAIRS

ROYALTY &
RELIGION

CELEBRITY

SCIENCE &
NATURE

SPORT &
LEISURE

ARTS, CULTURE
& MEDIA

A TWEET A DAY

GLOSSARY
& THANKS

— The Half-time Show —

Always a big part of the Super Bowl, the 2011 half-time show had the Black Eyed Peas providing the entertainment, going all out with hundreds of dancers, and guests Usher and Slash. Many of those tweeting at home, however, were distinctly unimpressed.

@fivethirtyeight Nate Silver
Turn on FOX -- really clever parody
of a Super Bowl halftime show.
6 Feb

@AntDeRosa Anthony De Rosa
I think we now know how to get Mubarak to leave.
6 Feb

@rgiraldi Richard Giraldi
God - never in my life have I wanted @kanyewest
to interrupt a performance more. #superbowl
#blackeyedpeas
6 Feb

@Mike_FTW Mike Monteiro
The Black Eyed Peas halftime show was possibly the worst 6 hours of television I've ever seen.
6 Feb

INTRO

POLITICS &
CURRENT AFFAIRS

ROYALTY &
RELIGION

CELEBRITY

SCIENCE &
NATURE

SPORT &
LEISURE

ARTS, CULTURE
& MEDIA

A TWEET A DAY

GLOSSARY
& THANKS

—— Tweeting the Commercials ——

No rest for the tweeters: the annual sport of dissecting the Super Bowl adverts keeps the commentary running through the breaks in play.

@BorowitzReport Andy Borowitz
#SuperBowl I guess Groupon decided to do a funny commercial about Tibet because Darfur would be in bad taste? #AdFAIL
6 Feb

@andyhaynesed Andy Haynes
The next Groupon commercial covers how cheap hotels in Haiti are right now. #superbowl
6 Feb

@rohitbhargava Rohit Bhargava
Groupon seems to have achieved the unique feat of paying $3M to lose customers who previously loved them. #brandbowl
6 Feb

@elkgirl Laura R.
@Groupon Your commercials this eve were tactless. #unsubscribe #brandbowl
7 Feb

INTRO

POLITICS &
CURRENT AFFAIRS

ROYALTY &
RELIGION

CELEBRITY

SCIENCE &
NATURE

SPORT &
LEISURE

ARTS, CULTURE
& MEDIA

A TWEET A DAY

GLOSSARY
& THANKS

THE MOST POPULAR SUPER BOWL ADVERTS IN THE TWITTERSPHERE

Doritos	33,930 tweets, 6% positive
Chrysler	32,514 tweets, 16.5% positive
VW	25,674 tweets, 32.1% positive
Pepsi Max	23,726 tweets, 5.8% positive
Best Buy	18,722 tweets, 9.6% positive

Source: Brandbowl2011.com, Radian6.com and Mullon.com

—— National Marijuana Day ——

The date of this annual 'holiday' in the USA (20 April) was, according to lore, chosen to reflect smokers' preferred time for lighting up: 4.20 p.m.

> **@SteveMartinToGo** Steve Martin
> Today is National Marijuana Day. A day when…uh…wow, Wolf Blitzer is SO funny.
> 20 Apr

@ApocalypseHow Rob Kutner
"What if we're ALL just Tweets on some giant being's Twitter feed…?" #happy420
20 Apr

@Tyga_YMCMB #TeamTYGA
4/20 is national weed day, 4/21 is national random Drug test day.
20 Apr

INTRO

POLITICS &
CURRENT AFFAIRS

ROYALTY &
RELIGION

CELEBRITY

SCIENCE &
NATURE

SPORT &
LEISURE

ARTS, CULTURE
& MEDIA

A TWEET A DAY

GLOSSARY
& THANKS

6,303

TPS when Wayne Rooney scored for
Manchester United against Barcelona during
the UEFA Champions League final on
28 May 2011. At the time it was the
second highest spike ever recorded

Source: Twitter

— 1 JULY 2011 —

WIMBLEDON: MURRAY VS NADAL

No Briton has won the Men's Singles title at Wimbledon
since Fred Perry in 1936, but in 2011 Scotsman Andy
Murray, the number four seed, looked like he was in with a
chance. His Spanish opponent, reigning champion Rafael
Nadal, wasn't going to relinquish the title without a fight.

Note: All times local to UK

@sarahrainey4 Sarah Rainey
Just met a woman who has queued for Wimbledon
ground passes 37 YEARS IN A ROW. Must be 5,000 people
on Henman Hill today. Mad #wimbledon
3.54 p.m. 1 Jul

INTRO

POLITICS &
CURRENT AFFAIRS

ROYALTY &
RELIGION

CELEBRITY

SCIENCE &
NATURE

SPORT &
LEISURE

ARTS, CULTURE
& MEDIA

A TWEET A DAY

GLOSSARY
& THANKS

@Mike_Dickson_DM Mike Dickson
Murray is doing absolutely everything he should be.
Aggressive, serving great. Heading for tiebreak.
4.33 p.m. 1 Jul

@OfficiallyGT Georgie Thompson
*Somebody got out the right side
of the bed this morning!
Murray looking unbeatable.*
5.44 p.m. 1 Jul

@suntimesbazzaf Barry Flatman
Suddenly @andy_murray let's intensity slip. Double fault
& slack overhead equals service break for Rafa
6.01 p.m. 1 Jul

@suntimesbazzaf Barry Flatman
How quick a momentum switch can change things.
@andy_murray broken twice in succession. Trails 5-2
in 2nd
6.09 p.m. 1 Jul

@clarebalding1 Clare Balding
Right, History, take your hand off Murray's bloody
shoulder. It's messing with his serve. Nadal with double
break leads 5-2 second set
6.09 p.m. 1 Jul

@carolinecheese Caroline Cheese
Murray struggling with the hip injury. I'm not the only
one seeing that right? I'm already starting to think about
US Open #doommonger
6.09 p.m. 1 Jul

INTRO

POLITICS &
CURRENT AFFAIRS

ROYALTY &
RELIGION

CELEBRITY

SCIENCE &
NATURE

SPORT &
LEISURE

ARTS, CULTURE
& MEDIA

A TWEET A DAY

GLOSSARY
& THANKS

125,640

Number of mentions of
Murray on 1 July 2011

Source: Research.ly

115,330

Number of mentions of
Nadal on 1 July 2011

@suntimesbazzaf Barry Flatman
Nadal levels at one set all. Concern how @andy_murray
let his grasp slip so quickly
6.15 p.m. 1 Jul

@SazzyMCH Sarah Hamilton
*The magic button — Make Everything
OK make-everything-ok.com
<<Worth a try right?!?*
6.38 p.m. 1 Jul

@carolinecheese Caroline Cheese
Nadal 2 sets to 1 up v Murray. Let's be honest, it'd be
much better if Murray won his 1st #Wimbledon in
Olympics year img.ly/5loz
6.49 p.m. 1 Jul

@DiscoDebMKE Deb
Hey British Press - I understand you'll be upset, but let's
not be ruthless. #Wimbledon #keepittogether
7.33 p.m. 1 Jul

INTRO

POLITICS &
CURRENT AFFAIRS

ROYALTY &
RELIGION

CELEBRITY

SCIENCE &
NATURE

SPORT &
LEISURE

ARTS, CULTURE
& MEDIA

A TWEET A DAY

GLOSSARY
& THANKS

@Alex_Kay_DM ALEX KAY
And Murray reaches his first Wimbledon final, destroying
Nadal in four sets. Oh, wait...
7.42 p.m. 1 Jul

@alex_willis Alexandra Willis
Oh Andy. #heartbreak
7.43 p.m. 1 Jul

91,321

Peak number of mentions of
Wimbledon in 2011 – on the
final day, 3 July

Source: Research.ly

—— 2 JULY 2011 ——

THE TOUR DE FRANCE

This year, the gruelling three-week race was marred by
some particularly nasty crashes, caused by cars, motorbikes
and spectators getting in the way of the cyclists. Over 3,430
km long, the race consisted of 21 stages over 23 days, with
198 riders competing in 22 teams. They narrated their
own journey.

Note: All times local to France

— Who's Who —

MARK CAVENDISH: British, team HTC-Highroad

ALBERTO CONTADOR: Spanish, team Saxo Bank-SunGard

CADEL EVANS: Australian, BMC Racing Team

JAKOB FUGSLANG: Danish, team Leopard Trek

GEORGE HINCAPIE: American, BMC Racing Team

DAVID MILLAR: British, team Garmin-Cervélo

MANUEL QUINZIATO: Italian, BMC Racing Team

MARK RENSHAW: Australian, team HTC-Highroad

FRÄNK SCHLECK: Luxembourg, team Leopard Trek

LAURENS TEN DAM: Dutch, team Rabobank

GERAINT THOMAS: British, team Sky

FREDERIK WILLEMS: Belgian, team Omega Pharma-Lotto

DAVID ZABRISKIE: American, team Garmin-Cervélo

@MarkCavendish Mark Cavendish
Well, IT's arrived! Thank you everyone for the messages of support. We'll do our best to make our fans proud. HERE. WE. GO.
9.57 a.m. 2 Jul

INTRO

POLITICS &
CURRENT AFFAIRS

ROYALTY &
RELIGION

CELEBRITY

SCIENCE &
NATURE

SPORT &
LEISURE

ARTS, CULTURE
& MEDIA

A TWEET A DAY

GLOSSARY
& THANKS

@Mark_Renshaw Mark Renshaw

Thanks to all the spectator's who didnt stand on the road today. All you people who did, your bloody crazy! Stand back please... Thankyou

6.36 p.m. 2 Jul

@GeraintThomas86 Geraint Thomas

214km down, 3216km to go...

10.15 p.m. 3 Jul

@jakob_fuglsang Jakob Fuglsang

Thank God Im alive & in one piece! Stupidest stage I've ever done!! @ASO this was not okay. Hope that nobody are hurt to bad!

6.05 p.m. 6 Jul

@albertocontador Alberto Contador

Thanks for your interest. I'm fine after the fall. Now with ice throughout the body, I'll pass not a good night, but tomorrow all out...:)

7.20 p.m. 6 Jul

64%
Increase in followers of yellow-jersey (overall) winner, Cadel Evans, from 2 to 24 July

Source: TwitterCounter.com

49%
Increase in followers of green-jersey (points) winner, Mark Cavendish, from 2 to 24 July

@dzabriskie David Zabriskie
One time while self administering a colonic I think I saw Jesus...that is how I feel right now at this very moment...
6.25 p.m. 7 Jul

@CadelOfficial Cadel Evans
That was nuts....nursed through 226km of crashes to nearly get flattened by race security after the line.
#anotherdayattheoffice #TdF
6.46 p.m. 8 Jul

@manuelquinziato Manuel Quinziato
Just hope that the car driver who crashed Flecha and Hoogerland will be no more driving at a bike race in his whole life! #shame
7.26 p.m. 10 Jul

@millarmind David Millar
The seat next to me on the bus ride home was eerily empty. Shocking witnessing DZ flip the barrier. Missing the nutbag already. He's ok.
8.16 p.m. 10 Jul

@manuelquinziato Manuel Quinziato
I feel sorry for all the guys who crashed today! Above all for my friend @willemsfrederik who broke a collarbone!
8.26 p.m. 10 Jul

@albertocontador Alberto Contador
Tough day with another fall!Not very spectacular,but the blow in my right knee worries me.I'll rest a lot!
8.41 p.m. 10 Jul

INTRO

POLITICS & CURRENT AFFAIRS

ROYALTY & RELIGION

CELEBRITY

SCIENCE & NATURE

SPORT & LEISURE

ARTS, CULTURE & MEDIA

A TWEET A DAY

GLOSSARY & THANKS

INTRO

POLITICS &
CURRENT AFFAIRS

ROYALTY &
RELIGION

CELEBRITY

SCIENCE &
NATURE

SPORT &
LEISURE

ARTS, CULTURE
& MEDIA

A TWEET A DAY

GLOSSARY
& THANKS

@schleckfrank fränk schleck
I have no words to describe this day.need to have a sleep
than 2morrow I may have some words.
8.54 p.m. 10 Jul

@willemsfrederik Frederik Willems
After a ride of 10h in the ambulance. Almost in the
hospital of Herentals.nearly dead!! http://yfrog.com/
khqabtyj
10.54 p.m. 11 Jul

@GeraintThomas86 Geraint Thomas
1,916km done. 1,514km to go...
6.24 p.m. 13 Jul

@GeraintThomas86 Geraint Thomas
*Just been informed that the Tour 'really'
starts tomorrow... Well what the hell have
I been doing the last week n half?!*
7.13 p.m. 13 Jul

@MarkCavendish Mark Cavendish
Well, they've started. Mountains. #marvellous
8.43 p.m. 14 Jul

@millarmind David Millar
Thought I'd recovered well from todays mountain
gallivant until sat for dinner & @ChristianVDV said 'Wow,
your face is swollen.' Nice one.
12.28 a.m. 17 Jul

INTRO

POLITICS &
CURRENT AFFAIRS

ROYALTY &
RELIGION

CELEBRITY

SCIENCE &
NATURE

SPORT &
LEISURE

ARTS, CULTURE
& MEDIA

A TWEET A DAY

GLOSSARY
& THANKS

@CadelOfficial Cadel Evans
Little bit too much drama for me today.....Incredible
crowds-ears just stopped ringing! @BMCProTeam boys
are my heroes (again) #TdF
7.03 p.m. 22 Jul

@manuelquinziato Manuel Quinziato
In case you missed it: we fucking win the Tour de France!
9.38 p.m. 24 Jul

—— Tweeting without Thinking ——

Racist, sexist, jingoistic and just plain nasty trending topics
and hashphrases frequently clog up the trending topics list.
Four hours after the Women's World Cup between Japan
and the USA, 'Japs' and 'Pearl Harbor' were still lodged
at numbers eight and 10 on the trending topics list for the
US, although 'Congrats Japan' was at number four.

7,196

The record-breaking number of TPS at the
FIFA Women's World Cup final on
17 July 2011, when Japan beat
the United States

Source: Twitter

7,166

The second highest number of TPS at the
time, recorded at the Copa América final
on 24 July 2011, when Brazil
lost to Paraguay

INTRO

POLITICS &
CURRENT AFFAIRS

ROYALTY &
RELIGION

CELEBRITY

SCIENCE &
NATURE

SPORT &
LEISURE

ARTS, CULTURE
& MEDIA

A TWEET A DAY

GLOSSARY
& THANKS

— The Most-followed Pets —

TWEETER	USERNAME	FOLLOWERS
Sockington, cat	@sockington	1,477,104
Frankie, dog	@Frankie_Wah	31,482
Satsugai, cat	@SatsugaiCat	21,988
Tobias, cat	@FollowCat	18,229
Fluffy, cat	@fluffythecat	16,141
Stanley Pinkerton, dog	@mr_pinkerton	10,153
Romeo, cat	@romeothecat	9,898
Johann, dog	@JohannTheDog	9,041
Erica's Fish, fish	@ericasfish	8,288
Chloe, cat	@ChloeWaterDog	7,335

PROFILE:
@sockington

TWITTER BIO: 'I am Jason Scott's Cat'

FULL NAME: Sockington

BORN: Unknown

PROFESSION: Layabout

BACK STORY: Adopted from the street in Boston,
Massachusetts

NUMBER OF TWITTER USERS HE FOLLOWS: 888

AVERAGE TWEETS PER DAY: 1

AVERAGE FOLLOWERS ADDED PER DAY: Losing roughly 30

IMPACT SCORE: 23.6%

INFLUENCE SCORE: 5.7%

TWEET STYLE: Updates on a typical day of sleeping, scratching furniture, eating, attempting ill-advised jumps, complaining about what's on TV; lots of caps-lock confusion

IN HIS OWN WORDS:

sockington Sockamillion
WHAT'S THAT why am I waiting by the food dish OH NO REASON
18 Oct

sockington Sockamillion
OH GOD SOMEONE WANTS TO PET ME engage escape pod ESCAPE POD CONSISTS OF SHEDDING FUR escape pod not working
14 Mar

sockington Sockamillion
THIS JUST IN dining room intact DAMAGE MINIMAL hey don't go in there MY REPORT SHOULD HAVE BEEN SUFFICIENT
12 Jun

@sockington Sockamillion
SLEEPING ON THE DESK CHAIR TODAY don't understand why everyone says working at a desk is so hard THIS IS CAKE
2 Aug

INTRO

POLITICS & CURRENT AFFAIRS

ROYALTY & RELIGION

CELEBRITY

SCIENCE & NATURE

SPORT & LEISURE

ARTS, CULTURE & MEDIA

A TWEET A DAY

GLOSSARY & THANKS

INTRO

POLITICS &
CURRENT AFFAIRS

ROYALTY &
RELIGION

CELEBRITY

SCIENCE &
NATURE

SPORT &
LEISURE

ARTS, CULTURE
& MEDIA

A TWEET A DAY

GLOSSARY
& THANKS

6%

Pet dogs in the USA with a
Twitter account

*Source: lab42.com and
doggyloot.com*

— How Pets Tweet —

@FluffyTheCat Kitty Cat
Meow...
15 Jan

@ericasfish Erica's Fish
Pure stress in this house: the feeble chatter about
dinner and taxes, the meowing, the prancing about
of uncoordinated limbs.
15 Apr

@FollowCat Tobias
My favorite places to hide - under the bed, behind
the toilet, corner of the closet or anywhere in
Pakistan.
7 May

@Frankie_Wah Frankie
WE R DOGS dogs is waht we R WE WANT NUTHIN
MORE THAN TO LOVE U 4 EVER & ruin all your
material possessions
6 Jun

— The Most-followed Chefs —

TWEETER	USERNAME	FOLLOWERS
Jamie Oliver, UK	@jamieoliver	1,466,287
Bethenny Frankel, US	@Bethenny	622,461
Anthony Bourdain, US	@NoReservations	527,814
Paula Deen, US	@Paula_Deen	501,539
Gordon Ramsay, UK	@GordonRamsay01	417,005
Guy Fieri, US	@GuyFieri	388,548
Giada De Laurentiis, Italy/US	@GDeLaurentiis	387,468
Bobby Flay, US	@bflay	336,614
Rachael Ray, US	@rachael_ray	307,853
Tyler Florence, US	@TylerFlorence	306,119

PROFILE:
@jamieoliver

TWITTER BIO: 'The Official Jamie Oliver twitter page'

FULL NAME: James Trevor Oliver

BORN: 27 May 1975 in Clavering, Essex

PROFESSION: Chef, cookbook author, campaigner for healthy eating

BACK STORY: Rose to fame in 1997 with his cooking show *The Naked Chef*, which celebrated his slapdash

INTRO

POLITICS & CURRENT AFFAIRS

ROYALTY & RELIGION

CELEBRITY

SCIENCE & NATURE

SPORT & LEISURE

ARTS, CULTURE & MEDIA

A TWEET A DAY

GLOSSARY & THANKS

INTRO

POLITICS &
CURRENT AFFAIRS

ROYALTY &
RELIGION

CELEBRITY

SCIENCE &
NATURE

SPORT &
LEISURE

ARTS, CULTURE
& MEDIA

A TWEET A DAY

GLOSSARY
& THANKS

style and cockney accent. Set up the Fifteen
Foundation in 2002, which trained disadvantaged
young people as chefs, and was awarded an MBE
in 2003. Campaigned to improve school dinners in
the UK and USA with TV shows in both countries.
Now owns a chain of restaurants. Married with
four children.

NUMBER OF TWITTER USERS HE FOLLOWS: 4,174

AVERAGE TWEETS PER DAY: 2

AVERAGE FOLLOWERS ADDED PER DAY: 2,700. Passed
the 1 million mark in March 2011

IMPACT SCORE: 77.6%

INFLUENCE SCORE: 78.7%

TWEET STYLE: Very friendly – frequently responds to
his followers' cooking questions

Twitter and Romance May Not Go Hand in Hand

According to a 2011 survey by dating website OkCupid,
people who use Twitter every day have shorter relation-
ships. It's impossible, however, to tell who's doing the
breaking up, so the issue of whether regular tweeters have
shorter attention spans or are just plain annoying is still in
question.

— 6 —

ARTS, CULTURE & MEDIA

@LiterallyJamie Not Jamie Redknapp
Bono + electrical equipment + rain.
Science - don't fail me now. #glasto
10.17 p.m. 24 Jun

INTRO

POLITICS &
CURRENT AFFAIRS

ROYALTY &
RELIGION

CELEBRITY

SCIENCE &
NATURE

SPORT &
LEISURE

ARTS, CULTURE
& MEDIA

A TWEET A DAY

GLOSSARY
& THANKS

— The Most-followed Comedians —

TWEETER	USERNAME	FOLLOWING
Jimmy Fallon, US	@jimmyfallon	4,046,011
Chelsea Handler, US	@ChelseaHandler	3,854,208
Conan O'Brien, US	@conanobrien	3,716,672
Daniel Tosh, US	@danieltosh	3,244,775
Russell Brand, UK	@rustyrockets	3,017,409
Stephen Fry, UK	@stephenfry	3,008,833
Rafinha Bastos, Brazil	@rafinhabastos	2,928,525
Justin Halpern, US	@shitmydadsays	2,608,865
Stephen Colbert, US	@stephenathome	2,581,036
Marco Luque, Brazil	@marcoluque	2,468,760
Joel McHale, Canada/US	@joelmchale	2,281,962
Bill Cosby, US	@billcosby	2,170,227
Al Yankovic, US	@alyankovic	2,125,615
Sarah Silverman, US	@sarahksilverman	2,062,972
Eddie Izzard, UK	@eddieizzard	2,013,072
Danilo Gentili, Brazil	@danilogentili	1,988,287
Dane Cook, US	@danecook	1,956,872
Kevin Hart, US	@KevinHart4real	1,927,151
Michael Ian Black, US	@michaelianblack	1,657,790
Steve Martin, US	@SteveMartinToGo	1,561,781

INTRO

POLITICS & CURRENT AFFAIRS

ROYALTY & RELIGION

CELEBRITY

SCIENCE & NATURE

SPORT & LEISURE

ARTS, CULTURE & MEDIA

A TWEET A DAY

GLOSSARY & THANKS

Arts, Culture & Media

If there's one thing that Twitter is great at, it's humour. No wonder, then, that comedians are among the most followed. Non-professionals also get in on the act, providing whip-smart instant analysis on awards shows, from the Oscars to the Grammys, and witty reporting from festivals, such as Glastonbury. Watching TV with a second screen – whether a smart phone or laptop – so that you can follow the conversation about it on social media is increasingly becoming the norm. So much so, in fact, that it's helping to revive that old-fashioned concept of 'appointment TV' – watching a show when it's broadcast rather than recording it for later. After all, no one wants to discover what happened in an episode they've not yet seen from a trending topic. And for the rest of us, there are plenty of fictional characters and dead authors with Twitter feeds, plus one very fashionable elevator.

INTRO

POLITICS &
CURRENT AFFAIRS

ROYALTY &
RELIGION

CELEBRITY

SCIENCE &
NATURE

SPORT &
LEISURE

ARTS, CULTURE
& MEDIA

A TWEET A DAY

GLOSSARY
& THANKS

PROFILE:
@jimmyfallon

TWITTER BIO: 'Astrophysicist'

FULL NAME: James Thomas Fallon

BORN: 19 September 1974, Brooklyn, New York

PROFESSION: Comedian, actor and talk show host

BACK STORY: His big break came in 1999 when he
joined the team on the US sketch show *Saturday
Night Live*. He left in 2004, going on to star in
films, including *Fever Pitch* and *Whip It*, and then
took over as host of the talk show *Late Night*.
Twitter is a key part of the show: he tweets his
monologue jokes in advance, and announces
made-up hashphrases on air, showing his viewers'
best efforts on screen. He is married with no
children.

NUMBER OF TWITTER USERS HE FOLLOWS: 3,620

AVERAGE TWEETS PER DAY: 3

AVERAGE FOLLOWERS ADDED PER DAY: 4,600

IMPACT SCORE: 67.0%

INFLUENCE SCORE: 77.1%

TWEET STYLE: Lots of jokes and plenty of links to
funny videos and pictures

INTRO

POLITICS &
CURRENT AFFAIRS

ROYALTY &
RELIGION

CELEBRITY

SCIENCE &
NATURE

SPORT &
LEISURE

ARTS, CULTURE
& MEDIA

A TWEET A DAY

GLOSSARY
& THANKS

IN HIS OWN WORDS:

"

@jimmy fallon jimmy fallon
Let's play the hashtag game! Tweet something
embarrassing/crazy that happened at the beach and
tag with #beachfail. Could be on our show.
12 Jul

@jimmyfallon jimmy fallon
Fell asleep listening to my iPod. Woke up with a
headphone-cord tanline around my left nip. And no
iPod. #beachfail
12 Jul

@jimmyfallon jimmy fallon
Shark Week Fact #5: If a shark laughs too hard, it
will poop. #sharkfacts
6 Aug

"

— The Stephen Fry Effect —

One of the UK's best-loved celebrities, Fry is a comedian,
author, actor and game-show host whose influence over his
followers is now legendary. A single tweet recommending a
musician, book or website prompts such a response that his
own site carries a warning about asking for retweets: 'Very
few websites can manage that traffic.'

INTRO

POLITICS &
CURRENT AFFAIRS

ROYALTY &
RELIGION

CELEBRITY

SCIENCE &
NATURE

SPORT &
LEISURE

ARTS, CULTURE
& MEDIA

A TWEET A DAY

GLOSSARY
& THANKS

— 16 JANUARY 2011 —

RICKY GERVAIS SHOCKS
AT THE GOLDEN GLOBES

The British comedian pulled no punches when he hosted the Hollywood Foreign Press Association's film and TV awards ceremony.

Note: All times local to California

@suzemuse Susan Murphy
Ricky Gervais just called Bruce Willis "Ashton Kutcher's Dad". :)
5.22 p.m. 16 Jan

@rodfeuer Rod Feuer
robert downey jr humor > ricky gervais #goldenglobes
6.07 p.m. 16 Jan

@JewAmerPrincess Jewish Amer Princess
Poor Robert Downey Jr., was it really necessary for Ricky Gervais to call him out? Who in that room HASN'T had a drug problem? #goldenglobes
7.18 p.m. 16 Jan

@mfullilove Michael Fullilove
Ricky Gervais denies #GoldenGlobes judges only nominated "The Tourist" so they cd meet Jolie + Depp: "Rubbish, they also accepted bribes."
7.35 p.m. 16 Jan

INTRO

POLITICS & CURRENT AFFAIRS

ROYALTY & RELIGION

CELEBRITY

SCIENCE & NATURE

SPORT & LEISURE

ARTS, CULTURE & MEDIA

A TWEET A DAY

GLOSSARY & THANKS

@memimemimy caroline
Ricky Gervais, just ended the Golden Globes by saying:
"Thank you God for making me an atheist." I'm LMAO.
8.01 p.m. 16 Jan

@poniewozik James Poniewozik
More damaging to Gervais' future-hosting hopes:
mocking God or mocking Depp/Jolie? #RickyWatch2011
8.05 p.m. 16 Jan

@davecaughey Dave Caughey
If Charlie Sheen was offended by Ricky Gervais' joke at
the Golden Globes, he needs to get off his high whores.
5.49 a.m. 17 Jan

@JoEteson Jo Goldsmith Eteson
On one hand cringe worthy, uber awkward &
perhaps over the line... On the other, hilarious!
http://bit.ly/ePo2tF #goldenglobes #rickygervais
9:59 p.m. 17 Jan

— *Glee* at the Globes —

The three most tweeted moments during the Golden
Globes? All were about the same TV show: *Glee*. No
surprise, given the 30-fold increase in Twitter use during
the broadcast of an episode.

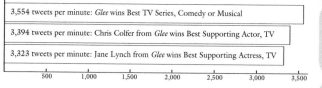

3,554 tweets per minute: *Glee* wins Best TV Series, Comedy or Musical

3,394 tweets per minute: Chris Colfer from *Glee* wins Best Supporting Actor, TV

3,323 tweets per minute: Jane Lynch from *Glee* wins Best Supporting Actress, TV

| 500 | 1,000 | 1,500 | 2,000 | 2,500 | 3,000 | 3,500 |

Sources: Tweetreach.com and Twitter

INTRO

POLITICS &
CURRENT AFFAIRS

ROYALTY &
RELIGION

CELEBRITY

SCIENCE &
NATURE

SPORT &
LEISURE

ARTS, CULTURE
& MEDIA

A TWEET A DAY

GLOSSARY
& THANKS

The Most-followed TV Shows, Newspapers and Magazines

TWEETER	USERNAME	FOLLOWING
The Ellen Show	@theellenshow	7,409,502
CNN Breaking News	@cnnbrk	4,958,188
The New York Times	@nytimes	3,630,037
Programa Panico	@programapanico	3,299,933
E Entertainment	@eonline	3,240,751
The Onion	@TheOnion	3,042,076
People Magazine	@peoplemag	2,828,587
Time Magazine	@time	2,794,848
CNN	@cnn	2,476,584
Funny Or Die	@funnyordie	2,353,472

— 13 FEBRUARY 2011 —

THE GRAMMYS

Surprises abounded at the annual music awards ceremony in Los Angeles. Lady Gaga arrived in an egg, revealing prosthetic horns and pointy shoulders when she hatched, while Justin Bieber's massive fanbase didn't help his cause with the Grammy voters.

Note: All times local to California

INTRO

POLITICS & CURRENT AFFAIRS

ROYALTY & RELIGION

CELEBRITY

SCIENCE & NATURE

SPORT & LEISURE

ARTS, CULTURE & MEDIA

A TWEET A DAY

GLOSSARY & THANKS

@pourmecoffee pourmecoffee
I'd be willing to sign something stipulating Lady Gaga is outrageous. I feel like it might take some pressure off her.
4.27 p.m. 13 Feb

@poniewozik James Poniewozik
People can rip on Gaga all they want, but that was a beautiful statement of support for all of us with shoulder horns. #grammys
5.31 p.m. 13 Feb

@rickmercer Rick Mercer
You know ur 40 when you google an artist on the Grammys bc you don't know them and they pop up on forbes highest paid list.
5.56 p.m. 13 Feb

@biebercruz SWAG BELIEBER
Omfg justin deserved it so much that girl just came outta no where n stole it! Stupid grammy ppl chosin ppl who dont deserve it
7.26 p.m. 13 Feb

@BieberTeamNY JB♥NY
hey @espespalding congrats on winning best unknown artist!!!!!!!!!!!!!! u def deserved that one
7.46 p.m. 13 Feb

INTRO

POLITICS &
CURRENT AFFAIRS

ROYALTY &
RELIGION

CELEBRITY

SCIENCE &
NATURE

SPORT &
LEISURE

ARTS, CULTURE
& MEDIA

A TWEET A DAY

GLOSSARY
& THANKS

@BieberFansFL Live. Love. Belieъ
WHO THE HELL IS ARCADE FIRE?! Its official, the
grammys is a joke
8.24 p.m. 13 Feb

17,000

Peak number of tweets per minute
during the Grammys

Source: TweetReach.com

—— Twitter Predicts the Grammys? ——

If your Twitter influence could win you awards, the results
would have been very different.

CATEGORY	MOST INFLUENCE ON TWITTER	REAL WINNER
Record of the Year	*Love the Way You Lie* Eminem featuring Rihanna	*Need You Now* Lady Antebellum
Album of the Year	*The Fame Monster* Lady Gaga	*The Suburbs* Arcade Fire
Best New Artist	Justin Bieber	Esperanza Spalding

Source: Klout.com

The Most-followed Musicians

TWEETER	USERNAME	FOLLOWERS
Lady Gaga	@ladygaga	12,948,132
Justin Bieber	@justinbieber	12,164,201
Katy Perry	@katyperry	9,389,630
Britney Spears	@britneyspears	9,188,247
Shakira	@shakira	7,943,258
Taylor Swift	@taylorswift13	7,684,470
Rihanna	@rihanna	7,095,897
Selena Gomez	@selenagomez	6,988,721
Justin Timberlake	@jtimberlake	5,800,528
Eminem	@eminem	5,556,421
Nicki Minaj	@nickiminaj	5,284,052
Ashley Tisdale	@ashleytisdale	4,970,488
Pink	@pink	4,930,515
50 Cent	@50cent	4,890,210
Mariah Carey	@MariahCarey	4,754,887
Jessica Simpson	@jessicasimpson	4,029,854
Alicia Keys	@aliciakeys	4,335,382
Demi Lovato	@ddlovato	4,154,040
Coldplay	@coldplay	4,098,935
P Diddy	@iamdiddy	3,986,463

INTRO

POLITICS &
CURRENT AFFAIRS

ROYALTY &
RELIGION

CELEBRITY

SCIENCE &
NATURE

SPORT &
LEISURE

ARTS, CULTURE
& MEDIA

A TWEET A DAY

GLOSSARY
& THANKS

INTRO

POLITICS &
CURRENT AFFAIRS

ROYALTY &
RELIGION

CELEBRITY

SCIENCE &
NATURE

SPORT &
LEISURE

ARTS, CULTURE
& MEDIA

A TWEET A DAY

GLOSSARY
& THANKS

— 27 FEBRUARY 2011 —
THE ACADEMY AWARDS

Aside from the winners, it's the choice of dresses that provides the most controversy at the Oscars. This time, however, it was the choice of presenters: actors Anne Hathaway and James Franco. The latter, who is also a film director, screenwriter, author, painter and PhD student, tweeted during the ceremony; his (now closed) account was the second most mentioned after the Oscars' own account, @TheAcademy. Twitter's review? Not great…

Note: All times local to California

@MeetJamesFranco Nika Mavrody
Okay, you guys are right. James Franco is really bad at this.
6.46 p.m. 27 Feb

@Ali_Stephenson_ Ali Stephenson
Twitter abundant with desperate cries for Gervais.. Hathaway, Franco just aren't cutting the Oscars mustard it seems.. Boredom is knocking
7.01 p.m. 27 Feb

@ebertchicago Roger Ebert
I hope James Franco does better on the oral exam for his PhD.
7.05 p.m. 27 Feb

@TJMannixNYC T.J. Mannix
They are having to re-edit the Death Reel to include James Franco's career.
7.11 p.m. 27 Feb

@SimonJCLeBON Simon Le Bon
wot is the name of the ventriloquist dummy who's standing next to Anne Hathaway?
8.13 p.m. 27 Feb

@TVDoneWright Adam Wright
So this should put an end to James Franco 's endless schedule streak. Right? #Oscars
8.41 p.m. 27 Feb

11,780
Peak tweets per minute during ceremony, when Oprah Winfrey presented the award for Best Documentary Feature to the makers of *Inside Job*

Source: TweetReach.com

10,776
Second highest tweets per minute, when Melissa Leo said 'fuck' while accepting the award for Best Supporting Actress for her role in *The Fighter*

The Most Retweeted Tweet of the Oscars

@TheOnion The Onion
How rude — not a single character from Toy Story 3 bothered to show up. #oscars
27 Feb

Source: TweetReach.com

INTRO

POLITICS & CURRENT AFFAIRS

ROYALTY & RELIGION

CELEBRITY

SCIENCE & NATURE

SPORT & LEISURE

ARTS, CULTURE & MEDIA

A TWEET A DAY

GLOSSARY & THANKS

INTRO

POLITICS &
CURRENT AFFAIRS

ROYALTY &
RELIGION

CELEBRITY

SCIENCE &
NATURE

SPORT &
LEISURE

ARTS, CULTURE
& MEDIA

A TWEET A DAY

GLOSSARY
& THANKS

388,717

Total users tweeting
about the Oscars

Source: TweetReach.com

1,269,970

Total tweets relating to the Oscars
(excluding mentions of specific
films or celebrities)

— Twitter Predicts the —
Winners. Sort of…

By analysing both the volume and positivity of tweets
about the nominees, social media experts broke down who
the Twitterverse wanted to win. The results? Hit and miss.

CATEGORY	MOST TWEETS	MOST POSITIVE SENTIMENT	REAL WINNER
Best Actor	James Franco	Colin Firth	Colin Firth
Best Actress	Natalie Portman	Annette Bening	Natalie Portman

Source: Waggener Edstrom

INTRO

POLITICS &
CURRENT AFFAIRS

ROYALTY &
RELIGION

CELEBRITY

SCIENCE &
NATURE

SPORT &
LEISURE

ARTS, CULTURE
& MEDIA

A TWEET A DAY

GLOSSARY
& THANKS

— 4 MARCH 2011 —

CHRISTIAN DIOR SHOW

The fashion world was stunned when John Galliano, the designer behind his own-name label as well as Christian Dior, was arrested in Paris on an assault charge and videoed drunkenly making anti-Semitic remarks. Days later he was fired by Dior, but the show went on. The Jewish owner of the company, Bernard Arnault, did not attend (although his children did), while model Jessica Stam was one of those who was explicit in her support of the designer, and not just the brand. He was later convicted and apologised.

Note: All times local to France

@derekblasberg Derek Blasberg
Dior's Sydney Toledano has come out before the show to address the current uncommon circumstances of the house. Its the right thing to do.
3.08 p.m. 4 Mar

@susiebubble susiebubble
I feel awful at Dior right now...
3.08 p.m. 4 Mar

@Jeanne_Beker Jeanne Beker
Galliano at his best!!! The applause and cheering are bittersweet! Clapping continues for finale
3.23 p.m. 4 Mar

195

INTRO

POLITICS &
CURRENT AFFAIRS

ROYALTY &
RELIGION

CELEBRITY

SCIENCE &
NATURE

SPORT &
LEISURE

ARTS, CULTURE
& MEDIA

A TWEET A DAY

GLOSSARY
& THANKS

@vogue_london VOGUE.COM UK
Entire dior team, 40ish people, take a bow at Dior - all wearing white lab jackets, audience all cheering them #pfw -dj
3.27 p.m. 4 Mar

@derekblasberg Derek Blasberg
I applaud Dior today. By acknowledging their crisis and reminding us that Dior is more than a single man, they prove the house will survive.
3.35 p.m. 4 Mar

@LorraineELLE Lorraine Candy
Dior: strangely moving show. Tribute to the brand.
3.42 p.m. 4 Mar

@vogue_london VOGUE.COM UK
Some school children begged for my ticket outside Dior. I gave in + they ran off screaming in joy. Hope they make millions with it #pfw -dj
3.45 p.m. 4 Mar

@Jess_Stam Jessica Stam
I believe every human being on this earth was created equal. I also don't turn my back on my friends when they're in a dark place #Galliano
5.17 p.m. 4 Mar

The Most-followed Media Personalities

TWEETER	USERNAME	FOLLOWERS
Oprah Winfrey, US	@Oprah	6,949,444
Ryan Seacrest, US	@RyanSeacrest	4,944,406
Chelsea Handler, US	@chelseahandler	3,763,272
Tyra Banks, US	@tyrabanks	3,706,378
Perez Hilton, US	@PerezHilton	3,678,907
Rafinha Bastos, Brazil	@rafinhabastos	2824097
Stephen Colbert, US	@stephenathome	2,539,810
Nicole Polizzi, US	@sn00ki	2,533,206
Dr Drew Pinsky, US	@DrDrew	2,372,230
Martha Stewart, US	@MarthaStewart	2,319,600
Giuliana Rancic, US	@GiulianaRancic	2,271,023
Marcos Mion, Brazil	@marcosmion	2,266,965
Rodrigo Scarpa, Brazil	@rodrigovesgo	2,161,771
Fearne Cotton, UK	@Fearnecotton	1,997,850
Lauren Conrad, US	@LaurenConrad	1,993,508
Paula Abdul, US	@PaulaAbdul	1,989,714
Tony Robbins, US	@TonyRobbins	1,977,682
Larry King, US	@kingsthings	1,918,736
Marcelo Tas, Brazil	@marcelotas	1,910,611
Rachel Maddow, US	@maddow	1,906,823

INTRO

POLITICS & CURRENT AFFAIRS

ROYALTY & RELIGION

CELEBRITY

SCIENCE & NATURE

SPORT & LEISURE

ARTS, CULTURE & MEDIA

A TWEET A DAY

GLOSSARY & THANKS

INTRO

POLITICS &
CURRENT AFFAIRS

ROYALTY &
RELIGION

CELEBRITY

SCIENCE &
NATURE

SPORT &
LEISURE

ARTS, CULTURE
& MEDIA

A TWEET A DAY

GLOSSARY
& THANKS

PROFILE:
@Oprah

TWITTER BIO: 'Live Your Best Life'

FULL NAME: Oprah Gail Winfrey

BORN: 29 January 1954, rural Mississippi

PROFESSION: Talk show host (retired) and media mogul

BACK STORY: Born in poverty to a teenage mother, she is the ultimate rags-to-riches story. Forbes now estimates her net worth at $2.7 billion, thanks largely to her talk show, which ended in May 2011 after 25 years on air. Just as a mention on her TV show would catapult a book onto the bestseller list, so does a tweet: one recipient, @erinbury, added over 5,000 followers in a single day when she retweeted her. Winfrey lives with her long-term boyfriend, Stedman Graham.

NUMBER OF TWITTER USERS SHE FOLLOWS: 33

AVERAGE TWEETS PER DAY: 5

AVERAGE FOLLOWERS ADDED PER DAY: 11,000

IMPACT SCORE: 74.1%

INFLUENCE SCORE: 55.1%

TWEET STYLE: A rare tweeter until spring 2011, she now rewards her loyal followers with links to candid videos of herself at home. Frequent mentions of both her fans and her celebrity friends.

INTRO

POLITICS &
CURRENT AFFAIRS

ROYALTY &
RELIGION

CELEBRITY

SCIENCE &
NATURE

SPORT &
LEISURE

ARTS, CULTURE
& MEDIA

A TWEET A DAY

GLOSSARY
& THANKS

— Oprah Winfrey's Last Show —

On 25 May 2011, after 25 years on air, the talk show queen retired her crown; some Twitter users saw the funny side.

"

@mikedrucker Mike Drucker
Haha, last Oprah audience: she's giving you the gift of inspiration and self-confidence. You lose.
25 May

@badbanana Tim Siedell
Disappointed in the Oprah finale. I was hoping the writers would explain Dr. Phil.
25 May

@teamyasumura Robert Yasumura
No one else thinks this Oprah ending thing is going to result in a mass suicide of middle aged women?
25 May

@seanoconnz sean oconnor
I'm going to miss Oprah, just like I've missed every episode up until now.
25 May

"

INTRO

POLITICS &
CURRENT AFFAIRS

ROYALTY &
RELIGION

CELEBRITY

SCIENCE &
NATURE

SPORT &
LEISURE

ARTS, CULTURE
& MEDIA

A TWEET A DAY

GLOSSARY
& THANKS

The Most-followed Dead Authors

TWEETER	USERNAME	FOLLOWERS
Kurt Vonnegut	@kurt_vonnegut	70,667
Samuel Johnson	@DrSamuelJohnson	36,531
Mark Twain	@TheMarkTwain	31,894
Edgar Allen Poe	@Edgar_Allan_Poe	23,448
Samuel Pepys	@samuelpepys	17,979
Mark Twain	@TwainToday	15,154
J.R.R.Tolkein	@JRRTolkein	14,140
Laura Ingalls Wilder	@halfpintingalls	10,080
Henry David Thoreau	@ThoreauPage	6,848
William Shakespeare	@Wwm_Shakespeare	5,598

Dr Johnson Tweets

The opinionated 18th-century author of the first dictionary was born, it seems, for Twitter.

@DrSamuelJohnson Samuel Johnson
"Sir, didst thou mean hot Tea with Milk?"
"Madam, must I now specify brown Leaves with
Liquid Water & China RECEPTACLE?"
20 Jul

INTRO

POLITICS &
CURRENT AFFAIRS

ROYALTY &
RELIGION

CELEBRITY

SCIENCE &
NATURE

SPORT &
LEISURE

ARTS, CULTURE
& MEDIA

A TWEET A DAY

GLOSSARY
& THANKS

@DrSamuelJohnson Samuel Johnson
Brunch (n.) midday Repast for the mewling
Adult-Infant, too sap-liver'd to rise for Breakfast or
digest for LUNCHEON
24 Jul

@DrSamuelJohnson Samuel Johnson
The Reunification of Messrs BLACK SABBATH is both
gratifying for the West Midlands and portentous of
the APOCALYPSE
17 Aug

— 24 JUNE 2011 —

GLASTONBURY FESTIVAL

Despite its near synonymous association with mud, this
year the 41-year-old music festival on a farm in Somerset,
England, was attended by a reported 170,000 people.

Note: All times local to UK

@GlastoFest Glastonbury Festival
Please don't use the taps to clean your wellies - it's a real
waste of our water supplies (and it's unlikely they'll stay
clean). Thanks.
10.09 a.m. 24 Jun

@billybragg Billy Bragg
Morning chorus U2 soundchecking in the distance or at
least their roadies amping it up #glastonbury
10.14 a.m. 24 Jun

INTRO

POLITICS &
CURRENT AFFAIRS

ROYALTY &
RELIGION

CELEBRITY

SCIENCE &
NATURE

SPORT &
LEISURE

ARTS, CULTURE
& MEDIA

A TWEET A DAY

GLOSSARY
& THANKS

@caitlinmoran Caitlin Moran
The backstage area of Glastonbury now has a "Perrier Jouet delivery service" to your Winnebago, £120 *drinks supermarket brandy from flask*
2.10 p.m. 24 Jun

@SaliWho Sali Owen
Chumbawamba: "This song is about domestic violence." Some of the audience clap uncertainly. #Glasto
6.48 p.m. 24 Jun

@Ms_Dynamite Ms Dynamite
GLASTO WOW stage! TOO SICCCKKKKKKKKK 10,000 ppl tryin 2 cram in2 a 3000 capacity tent! NUTS! NRG! Xx
http://yfrog.com/h445337105j
7.24 p.m. 24 Jun

@LiterallyJamie Not Jamie Redknapp
Bono + electrical equipment + rain. Science - don't fail me now. #glasto
10.17 p.m. 24 Jun

@lindacolsh Linda Colsh
Jessie J (broken ankle? muddy faced) invites young singer on G'bury stage who does a fab job, knew every word & move! Well done!
4.49 p.m. 25 Jun

@jessiejofficial JESSIE J
Just left #glasto what an amazing show!!! So many people came out to watch!!! Loved it! I promised id bring some sun with me ;)
6.29 p.m. 25 Jun

INTRO

POLITICS &
CURRENT AFFAIRS

ROYALTY &
RELIGION

CELEBRITY

SCIENCE &
NATURE

SPORT &
LEISURE

ARTS, CULTURE
& MEDIA

A TWEET A DAY

GLOSSARY
& THANKS

@alexispetridis Alexis Petridis
Amazing comment on Sky News website story about the
guy that died at Glasto: "This is sad, but having a VIP
area at Glastonbury is sad too".
7.46 p.m. 26 Jun

@emilyeavis Emily Eavis
Thanks to you all for making it so special this year - truly
epic! A great send off.. See you in 2013 x
5.17p.m. 29 Jun

— Glasto by Numbers —

It may historically be all about rock music, but according
to a breakdown of 169,000 mentions of the festival on
Twitter, Beyoncé was the performer who ruled.

ARTIST	MENTIONS	ARTIST	MENTIONS
1. Beyoncé	19,969	11. Wu Tang	1,496
2. Coldplay	12,658	12. Primal Scream	1,482
3. U2	2,242	13. Tinie Temper	1,283
4. Radiohead	3,682	14. Paul Simon	1,163
5. Morrissey	3,352	15. Pendulum	936
6. Elbow	3,013	16. Plan B	881
7. Mumford & Sons	2,920	17. Fleet Foxes	822
8. BB King	2,105	18. Jessie J	789
9. Biffy Clyro	1,889	19. Vaccines	505
10. Chemical Brothers	1,701	20. Paolo Nutini	483

Source: Brandwatch.com

INTRO

POLITICS &
CURRENT AFFAIRS

ROYALTY &
RELIGION

CELEBRITY

SCIENCE &
NATURE

SPORT &
LEISURE

ARTS, CULTURE
& MEDIA

A TWEET A DAY

GLOSSARY
& THANKS

— Ai Weiwei Regains His Voice —

5 AUGUST 2011: A hugely prolific tweeter, the Chinese activist and artist Ai Weiwei was arrested at Beijing airport on 3 April 2011, ostensibly on charges of 'economic crimes'. After more than two months of detention, he was released on bail but banned from speaking to the media, and reportedly from using Twitter. It was August before he returned, with this much-retweeted understatement.

> **@aiww 艾未未 Ai Weiwei**
> 问个好吧。
> [*Alright*]
> 5 Aug

60,172

Number of tweets by
Ai Weiwei

Source: Twitter

The Most-followed Fictional Characters on Twitter

TWEETER	USERNAME	FOLLOWERS
Lord Voldemort, *Harry Potter*	@Lord_Voldemort7	1,694,547
Homer Simpson, *The Simpsons*	@HomerJSimpson	390,350
Darth Vader, *Star Wars*	@darthvader	360,234
Batman	@God_Damn_Batman	242,358
Death Star PR, *Star Wars*	@DeathStarPR	142,626
Drunk Hulk	@drunkhulk	105,516
Alan Partridge, *I'm Alan Partridge*	@ThisisPartridge	73,596
Feminist Hulk	@feministhulk	46,457
Peter Griffin, *Family Guy*	@PeterGriffin	35,921
Tracy Jordan, *30 Rock*	@TracyJordanTGS	23,755
Bender, *Futurama*	@Bender	23,578
Jerk Superman	@JerkSuperman	19,985
Han Solo, *Star Wars*	@hansolo	16,888
Don Draper, *Mad Men*	@don_draper	14,786
Dr Tobias Funke, *Arrested Development*	@drtobiasfunke	14,024
Stewie Griffin, *Family Guy*	@Stewie	12,390

INTRO

POLITICS & CURRENT AFFAIRS

ROYALTY & RELIGION

CELEBRITY

SCIENCE & NATURE

SPORT & LEISURE

ARTS, CULTURE & MEDIA

A TWEET A DAY

GLOSSARY & THANKS

INTRO

POLITICS &
CURRENT AFFAIRS

ROYALTY &
RELIGION

CELEBRITY

SCIENCE &
NATURE

SPORT &
LEISURE

ARTS, CULTURE
& MEDIA

A TWEET A DAY

GLOSSARY
& THANKS

PROFILE:
@Lord_Voldemort7

TWITTER BIO: 'I'm apparating in your windows.
Snatching your people up...'

FULL NAME: The Dark Lord, aka Tom Marvolo
Riddle, aka You Know Who

BORN: 30 June 1997, when the first in the Harry
Potter series of books was published

PROFESSION: Malevolence

BACK STORY: Abandoned, homicidal child turned
all-powerful wizard; spends his days plotting how
to achieve immortality and the destruction of the
human race; particularly obsessed with Twilight (in,
as you'd imagine, a bad way)

NUMBER OF TWITTER USERS HE FOLLOWS: 0

AVERAGE TWEETS PER DAY: 6

AVERAGE FOLLOWERS ADDED PER DAY: 4,900

IMPACT SCORE: 77.9%

INFLUENCE SCORE: 94.7%

TWEET STYLE: As menacing as you'd imagine,
with a healthy dose of humour; rarely resists the
opportunity to turn a trending hashphrase to his
advantage.

INTRO

POLITICS &
CURRENT AFFAIRS

ROYALTY &
RELIGION

CELEBRITY

SCIENCE &
NATURE

SPORT &
LEISURE

ARTS, CULTURE
& MEDIA

A TWEET A DAY

GLOSSARY
& THANKS

IN HIS OWN WORDS:

@Lord_Voldemort7 The Dark Lord
#50thingsIhate: people.
21 May

@Lord_Voldemort7 The Dark Lord
If at first you don't succeed, well maybe you're just stupid.
13 Jul

@Lord_Voldemort7 The Dark Lord
#riotcleanup. All I can say is #oops. Death Eaters misunderstood what a "flash mob" was. I was just trying to become Lord of the dance.
9 Aug

— The Condé Nast Elevator —

Home to *Vogue* and *GQ*, magazine publishing company Condé Nast also had a spy in its midst. A short-lived Twitter feed, based on conversations overheard in the lift, gave an insight into the cliché-ridden culture inside; by the time its author stopped tweeting, the account had reached 57,600 followers.

Note: All times local to New York

@CondeElevator Conde Elevator
Teen Vogue-er to Teen Vogue-er: "I don't understand why she was so pissed. I'd want to know if something made me look fat."
2.54 p.m. 7 Aug

INTRO

POLITICS &
CURRENT AFFAIRS

ROYALTY &
RELIGION

CELEBRITY

SCIENCE &
NATURE

SPORT &
LEISURE

ARTS, CULTURE
& MEDIA

A TWEET A DAY

GLOSSARY
& THANKS

@CondeElevator Conde Elevator
[silence] [silence] [silence] [silence]
[silence] [silence] [silence] [silence]
Summer Intern: "Was that...?"
Intern #2: "Yeah" #annawintour
4.43 p.m. 7 Aug

@CondeElevator Conde Elevator
Girl #1: I love that necklace, I saw it at Banana last
week and almost bought it too. Girl #2: [flips hair]
This is Gucci.
3.15 p.m. 8 Aug

@CondeElevator Conde Elevator
Lady #1: Well aren't you in a hurry? [air kisses] Lady #2:
[air kisses] My heli to East Hampton's leaving in 10!
3.31 p.m. 8 Aug

@CondeElevator Conde Elevator
[Guy walks into elevator wearing "Legalize Gay" t-shirt]
Teen Voguer: That shirt is so two months ago.
5.33 p.m. 8 Aug

@CondeElevator Conde Elevator
Summer Intern: My driver had SUCH a bad attitude. I was
like, "don't complain to me, I didn't eat lunch either! You
think I eat clothes?"
11.42 p.m. 10 Aug

A TWEET
A DAY

OCT
NOV
DEC
JAN
FEB
MAR
APR
MAY
JUN
JUL
AUG
SEP

— A Tweet a Day —

Presenting 12 months in the life of the Twitterverse, captured in 140 perfectly selected characters each day.

@Jenndepaula Jenn Hanson-dePaula
"Socializing on the Internet is to socializing what reality TV is to reality." I love you Aaron Sorkin...The Social Network... today!
1 Oct

@ConanOBrien Conan O'Brien
CNN's Rick Sanchez said the Jews run CNN. Ah, so that's who we blame for Rick Sanchez.
2 Oct

@pavolk Paul Kaye
Congratulations #Germany. Twentieth anniversary of #reunification. Great historical achievement. How long before #Korea manages same?
3 Oct

@bbc24 BBC News 24
Around 400 fans, celebrities, friends, and family members bid farewell to actor Tony Curtis at a funeral chapel in Las Vegas.
4 Oct

@louisedash Dr Louise Dash
Andre Geim first person to follow an IgNobel prize (2000, levitating frog) with #nobelprize #yakawow!
5 Oct

NOV

DEC

JAN

FEB

MAR

APR

MAY

JUN

JUL

AUG

SEP

@MikePasseri Mike Passeri
BREAKING NEWS: #Facebook is down. Worker productivity rises. U.S. climbs out of recession
6 Oct

@alandavies1 Alan Davies
Chilean miners coming up soon thankfully. Let's not miss this opportunity to HIDE.
7 Oct

@alexbracken Alexandra Bracken
Too cute: Johnny Depp Surprises Kids, Shows Up At School Dressed As Captain Jack
8 Oct

@BBCBreaking BBC Breaking News
Rescuers drill right through to the underground chamber where 33 miners have been trapped in Chile since August.
9 Oct

@hansolo Han Solo
Chewie has shaved his surprisingly ripped stomach and keeps referring to himself as the Sitchewation.
10 Oct

@ProfVolunteer stephanie gertz
Is it weird I'm sad about Courtney Cox & David Arquette?
11 Oct

@GiulianaRancic Giuliana Rancic
Hearing reports Christina Aguilera and husband split up. First Cox, now Ag? What the heck???
12 Oct

OCT
NOV
DEC
JAN
FEB
MAR
APR
MAY
JUN
JUL
AUG
SEP

@RyanSeacrest Ryan Seacrest
If ur just waking up, 12 miners have been rescued in Chile, 21 to go. AMAZING work from all involved!
13 Oct

@FATJEW The Fat Jew
I liked the Chilean Miners when they were still underground, now they're so mainstream
14 Oct

@kodyfrazier Kody Frazier
Top Gun 2 given the green light. Proving for the millionth time that Hollywood has no good ideas left....but yeah I'm totally gonna see it.
15 Oct

@Billboarddotcom Billboard
Congrats to @AliciaKeys and Swizz Beatz who welcomed their baby boy Egypt: http://bit.ly/a0rPZL
16 Oct

@ManzanitaGrunge Almis Power
Logra Iztapalapa Récord Guinness con enchilada más grande del mundo.... Luego porque dicen que ahí vive pura gente NICE.
[Iztapalapa achieves the Guinness World Record for the biggest enchilada... But then they say that people who live there are really NICE.]
17 Oct

@KeithKirkwood1 Keith Kirkwoodreal
A Happy Birthday Shout out to the Fred Astaire of Karate, The Muscles From Brussels Mr. Jean Claude Van Damme Happy 50th
18 Oct

OCT

NOV

DEC

JAN

FEB

MAR

APR

MAY

JUN

JUL

AUG

SEP

@mattround Matt Round
Cat bin lady was fined £250, precisely calculated by the judge to cancel out her You've Been Framed payment
19 Oct

In August 2010, a woman was caught on camera stroking a cat before dropping it into a rubbish bin, where it remained until its owners found it 15 hours later. Following a huge amount of publicity, the woman was identified as Mary Bale. She was prosecuted for causing unnecessary suffering to a cat, and apologised, saying she was 'profoundly sorry'.

@BBCBreaking BBC Breaking News
Chancellor George Osborne says budgets of every main UK government department to be cut by a third
20 Oct

@carelpedre Carel Pedre
#Cholera #Haiti last update: 1498 people affected... 134 deaths in 2 days ...
21 Oct

@wikileaks WikiLeaks
Pentagon says it expects 'nothing new' in next Wikileaks dump. 'Nothing new' to THEM goes without saying.
22 Oct

@morafi rafi
#wikileaks Iraq war: civilian deaths 66,081. That's one 9/11 every 4 months for the last 7 years. No monuments. No minutes silence.
23 Oct

@Thurnbs Thurnbs
Iraq war logs: US turned over captives to Iraqi torture squads
gu.com/p/2kjvt/tw via @guardian
24 Oct

@brenbeers Brendan Beers
Happy 25th anniversary Back to the Future. It has been a wild
ride. Now bring me my damn hoverboard.
25 Oct

@dat_Uschi Cathleen Keßler
Paul the Psychic Octopus died. He was buried today in a
private ceremony. There was a short reading followed by the
2014 World Cup results.
26 Oct

@sciam Scientific American
Extinction crisis revealed: One fifth of world's mammals, birds
and amphibians are threatened http://bit.ly/dariQL
27 Oct

@BreakingNews Breaking News
Sarah Palin tells Entertainment Tonight she'll run for president
in 2012 'if there's nobody else to do it' http://bit.ly/aKX8kN
28 Oct

@PhillipAMorton PhillipAndrewMorton
Mariah Carey pregnant. Potential baby names: Smurfette,
Ariel, Bambi, Hello Kitty.
29 Oct

@aman_tyagi Amandeep Tyagi
@Rally to restore Sanity. Some signs that people r holding r
really funny... "If Obama is Muslim, can we have Fridays off"
ahahahaha......
30 Oct

OCT

NOV

DEC

JAN

FEB

MAR

APR

MAY

JUN

JUL

AUG

SEP

@fotofobe Phoebe Sexton
Looks like I am going as a zombie barista this Halloween.
Didn't even have to shop for a costume. #LifeAfterGradSchool
31 Oct

@gabmeister1855 Gabriel Weinberger
We won the world series!!!!!!!!!!!!!!!!!!!!!!!!!!!!!!! #sfgiants
1 Nov

@twitter Twitter
Happy Election Day, America. Have you voted? If so, use the
tag #ivoted to get a badge in your tweet and remind others to
do their part.
2 Nov

@delrayser delrayser
Obama calls last night's results a "shellacking." Well,
a lot of Dems did see their seats varnish into thin air…
3 Nov

@liltunechi Lil Wayne
Aaaaaaahhhhhhmmmmm baaaaakkkkkkkkkk!
4 Nov

Eight months after he was sent to jail on a charge relating to a gun found on his tour bus, American rapper Lil
Wayne was released. This was the third most retweeted
tweet of 2010, according to Twitter.

@cmendler Camille Mendler
Happy #Diwali all. It coincides with Guy Fawkes Night (Nov 5)
here in UK. The fireworks displays will be HUGE!
5 Nov

@AJEnglish Al Jazeera English
Mexican drug cartel boss killed: Security forces shoot dead
suspected trafficking kingpin Tony the Storm.
http://aje.me/cNIIyS
6 Nov

@ACBreakingNews Asian Correspondent
Aussies plan referendum on Aboriginal recognition -
http://asiancorrespondent.com/breakingnews/aussies-plan-
referendum-on-aborigin.htm
7 Nov

@MandyGill Mandy Gill
Great day for TV (even though it's sunny out!) @ConanOBrien's
1st night back, and @Oprah has Michael Jackson's kids on!
8 Nov

@robdelaney rob delaney
George W. Bush's memoir,
Decision Points, comes out today!
#liar #murderer #liar #murderer #murder
#lying #lies #MURDER
9 Nov

@Reuters Reuters Top News
London student tuition fee protest turns violent as
demonstrators storm Conservative party headquarters
http://reut.rs/dl84Wt
10 Nov

@Mike2600 Mike Davis
R.I.P Dino de Laurentiis, producer of "Serpico," "Conan The
Barbarian," "Barbarella" and Giada de Laurentiis.
11 Nov

OCT
NOV
DEC
JAN
FEB
MAR
APR
MAY
JUN
JUL
AUG
SEP

OCT
NOV
DEC
JAN
FEB
MAR
APR
MAY
JUN
JUL
AUG
SEP

@crazycolours Crazy Colours
Crap! Robin Hood airport is closed. You've got a week to get your shit together, otherwise I'm blowing the airport sky high!! #IAmSpartacus
12 Nov

In May 2010, British man Paul Chambers was convicted of menace for sending a tweet to his friend @crazycolours, which threatened to blow up a UK airport closed by snow. The day after he lost his appeal in November, thousands (including @crazycolours above, who is now his fiancée) showed their support by retweeting the original message.

@lisaling lisaling
Aung San Suu Kyi freed after 15 years!!
13 Nov

@newssoverseas News Overseas
After 388 days Somali pirates released Paul and Rachel Chandler | NewsOverseas.com http://newsoverseas.com/?p=439
14 Nov

@rihanna Rihanna
Justin Bieber just flashed me his abs in the middle of a restaurant! Wow! He actually had a lil 6 pack! Sexy, lol! #Beliebersplzdontkillme
15 Nov

@ClarenceHouse Clarence House
The Prince of Wales is delighted to announce the engagement of Prince William to Miss Catherine Middleton
www.princeofwales.gov.uk
16 Nov

@Pink P!nk
My wish for this pregnancy, besides a healthy happy baby, is for the paparazzi to LEAVE US ALONE and let me gain my weight in PEACE. #mywish
17 Nov

@suppuser Nicolas Gosselin
International arrest warrant against Julian Assange, founder of Wikileaks, for sexual agression and rape.
18 Nov

@SamAtRedmag sam baker
Going to see new Harry Potter tonight. Don't even have kids to use as cover. #dontjudgeme
19 Nov

@GeekToMe Elliott Serrano
Pope says male prostitutes can justify using condoms. Guess I gotta start charging now for my 'services.' #doublewin #moneybackguarantee
20 Nov

@N1GHTFALL Jon Hague
Breaking News. Steve Jobs is to buy Ireland to solve the debt problem. It will be rebranded iLand #Bailout
21 Nov

@WorldVisionAus World Vision AUS
Over 300 people died in a stampede in #Cambodia after panic erupted at a water festival http://bit.ly/eMZvkF
22 Nov

@BrianO70 Brian Olsen
Tragic news today from the Pike River mine. No hope now of survivors. God how devistating for the families and friends
23 Nov

OCT
NOV
DEC
JAN
FEB
MAR
APR
MAY
JUN
JUL
AUG
SEP

@krishgm Krishnan Guru-Murthy
Sarah Palin hails her allies in...North Korea
http://thinkprogress.org/2010/11/24/palin-north-korea/
24 Nov

@bigshowfactoids BBC Radio 2 Factoids
The average weight of turkeys purchased for Thanksgiving
Dinner is 15 pounds.
25 Nov

@empiremagazine Empire Magazine
Look everyone! The first picture! From
Breaking Dawn! (Breathless fan reaction
simulated, on with the story):
http://bit.ly/fMxzzg
26 Nov

@vozdacomunidade Voz da Comunidade
Há 10 minutos atras foram ouvidos disparos aqui na
comunidade, segundo moradores os tiros são da favela da
Grota! #vozdacomunidade
[*10 minutes ago shots were heard here in the community,
residents said the shots are from the Grota slum!*]
27 Nov

As drug traffickers fought police in the slums of Rio
de Janeiro, 17-year-old journalism student Rene Silva
coralled other young locals and began tweeting what it
was like from the inside. Within a day, he had 20,000
followers.

@scottbeibin Scott Beibin
The next G20 is going to be soooooo awkward... #wikileaks
#cablegate
28 Nov

OCT
NOV
DEC
JAN
FEB
MAR
APR
MAY
JUN
JUL
AUG
SEP

@aluvious Alard von Westarp
Gotta love these @WikiLeaks guys, my fav: American diplomats labelled President Nicolas Sarkozy as the "emperor with no clothes". lmao
29 Nov

@alexmassie alexmassie
#wikileaks is probably not as good an organisation as its list of enemies would lead you to believe.
#stillausefulplacetostarthowever
30 Nov

@ABCtech ABC Tech & Games
Pakistan nuclear fears detailed by WikiLeaks http://myab.cc/gMFcSf #wikileaks #thestorythatjustkeepsongiving #cablegate
1 Dec

@Chris_Shallow Christopher Shallow
Boo Qatar. Damn it FIFA. 2018 World cup in Russia, 2022 in Qatar. #Fifa #Worldcup
2 Dec

@Julian_Ass Julian Ass
Not feeling myself today. Walked past a bag with a cat in it. Did nothing.
3 Dec

@UKuncut UK Uncut
Oxford Street stores shut down so far: Topshop, BHS, 2 x Dorothy Perkins, Boots, 2 x Vodafone and Miss Selfridge. Great work. #UKuncut
4 Dec

@keetredkid keith murdiff
UK Uncut targets Topshop and Vodafone over tax - gu.com/p/2yt8y/tw via @guardian- anyone know if a similar direct action group in Dublin?
5 Dec

OCT
NOV
DEC
JAN
FEB
MAR
APR
MAY
JUN
JUL
AUG
SEP

@DrSamuelJohnson Samuel Johnson
Jeremy HUNT (n.) Minister of the Crown or, according to
Mister NAUGHTIE, a Lady's Frontispiece http://bit.ly/hTCUNw
6 Dec

When James Naughtie, a presenter of BBC Radio 4's
agenda-setting news programme *Today*, introduced the
Culture Secretary, Jeremy Hunt, he accidentally trans-
posed two consonants. Twitter exploded in laughter, as
did he.

@arusbridger alan rusbridger
Assange refused bail, remanded in custody til Dec 14
#wikileaks
7 Dec

@LoniLove Loni Love
30 years after John Lennon's death more than 1 million people
in America have died due to hand gun crimes.. give peace a
chance
8 Dec

@AngieCrouch Angie Crouch
Students in London protesting tuition hikes attack car w/Prince
Charles and Camilla inside. Nobody hurt.
9 Dec

@BBCWorld BBC Global News
China criticises Nobel Committee for 'political theatrics'
after winning dissident's Prize placed on empty chair during
ceremony
10 Dec

OCT

NOV

DEC

JAN

FEB

MAR

APR

MAY

JUN

JUL

AUG

SEP

@carlbildt Carl Bildt
Most worrying attempt at terrorist attack in crowded part
of central Stockholm. Failed - but could have been truly
catastrophic..
11 Dec

@cnnbrk CNN Breaking News
Snow collapses #Metrodome roof in Minneapolis.
http://on.cnn.com/ehQnKI
12 Dec

@caitnightjokes Caitlin Tegart
Nicole Richie wore three dresses during her wedding to Joel
Madden, one for every year they'll be married.
13 Dec

@brundodecock Bruno Decock

14 Dec

@meropemills Merope
Inflation up, unemployment going that way, poss interest
rates rise soon and VAT increase in Jan. Economy not looking
so recovered today
15 Dec

@migueljmoran Miguel Moran
Time chooses Zuckerberg Person of the Year, 20 times less
voted than Mr. Assange. American media & Democracy..............
16 Dec

OCT

NOV

DEC

JAN

FEB

MAR

APR

MAY

JUN

JUL

AUG

SEP

@tlaquetzqui Chema
Bradley Manning, accused whistle-blower, turns 23 today in solitary confinement. Donate to his defense fund http://is.gd/iVv8n #Wikileaks
17 Dec

@BarackObama Barack Obama
By ending "Don't Ask, Don't Tell," no longer will patriotic Americans be asked to live a lie in order to serve the country they love.
18 Dec

@RamyRaoof Ramy Raoof
Sidi Bousid is burning http://nblo.gs/c1nhN background story on demonstations taking place in #SidiBouzid, #Tunisia by @linakhanum
19 Dec

@cancrime Rob Tripp
Top judge in England + Wales OKs tweeting from courtrooms http://bbc.in/hZm3O8 (thanx @KJjournalist)
20 Dec

@paddypower paddypower
Zara Phillips engaged - 1000/1 they save a few quid by a double wedding with Will & Kate!
21 Dec

@josanphoto Jo Ann Santangelo
Obama signing the end of #DADT! We can all serve open and honest http://www.youtube.com/watch?v=y0lg44azT2g #LGBT
22 Dec

@BorowitzReport Andy Borowitz
North Korea Threatens 'Holy War'; South Korea Responds with 'Holy Crap'
23 Dec

@Jemima_Khan Jemima Khan
(You've prob heard this but...) Dear Kids, There is no Santa. Those presents are from your parents. Love, Julian Assange - WikiLeaks
24 Dec

@loadedsanta Santa Claus
I just delivered 2 billion fucking presents FOR FREE across the world. But yeah, keep celebrating some other dude's birthday.
25 Dec

@CBSNews CBS News
Northeast Braces for Massive Blizzard - NYC could get 16 inches of snow with strong winds; D.C., Philly, Boston prepare http://bit.ly/hw0lbL
26 Dec

@CoryBooker Cory Booker
I'm in North now, I will get up there in a couple hrs RT @20perlz08: The seniors on Dover Street could use some shovelling. Thanks :)
12.53 p.m. 27 Dec

@samihtoukan Samih Toukan
Authorities in Tunisia are racing to block sites and facebook profiles and users are creating new ones...its cyber war #sidibouzid
28 Dec

@badbanana Tim Siedell
Holiday vacation. I have reached a level of inactivity normally associated with a Kardashian library card.
29 Dec

OCT
NOV
DEC
JAN
FEB
MAR
APR
MAY
JUN
JUL
AUG
SEP

OCT

NOV

DEC

JAN

FEB

MAR

APR

MAY

JUN

JUL

AUG

SEP

@AussieEllenFans Ellen Degeneres Fan
sympathies go out to all the families left stranded during the
christmas/new year floods in Queensland, Australia.
30 Dec

@KimJongil KimJongil
happy 1-1-11. I still hate you
31 Dec

@elliottyamin Elliott Yamin
Whoa!...its totally 2011 in japan right now!...happy new
year yall!
1 Jan

@joshgroban josh groban
On CNN...birds falling from the sky in alabama...100,000 fish
found dead in arkansas. Might be #timeforabucketlist
2 Jan

> **@stephenfry** Stephen Fry
> *The loss of the great Pete Postlethwaite*
> *is a very sad way to begin a year.*
> 3 Jan

@CharlesMBlow Charles M. Blow
Not sure how I feel about this Conrad Murray/Michael Jackson
murder trial. Michael was a junkie and Murray an enabler.
Everyone's at fault.
4 Jan

@TheHoxtonRaj Rajiv Desai
Aldershot striker Marvin Morgan placed on transfer list after
tweeting "I hope you all die" to fans who booed him - Ooops
5 Jan

@GOOD GOOD
Feel-good story of the day: Homeless man with amazing voice
gets a job http://su.pr/23zWu7
6 Jan

@JordanSekulow Jordan Sekulow
Southern Sudan Independence Referendum Sunday: Arab
Muslim North and the Black, Christian South
http://bit.ly/g6KOdD
7 Jan

@Rep_Giffords Gabrielle Giffords
My 1st Congress on Your Corner starts now.
Please stop by to let me know what is on
your mind or tweet me later.
8 Jan

@MMFlint Michael Moore
If a Detroit Muslim put a map on the web w/crosshairs on 20
pols, then 1 of them got shot, where would he
b sitting right now? Just asking.
9 Jan

@QPSmedia QPS Media Unit
Anyone living near Lockyer creek should IMMEDIATELY
evacuate to higher ground. #thebigwet #qldfloods
10 Jan

@paulverhoeven Paul Verhoeven
Saw picture of the guy rescuing a boatload of kangaroos
from the flooding. Now my mighty heart is breaking,
http://bit.ly/eMjSoG
11 Jan

OCT

NOV

DEC

JAN

FEB

MAR

APR

MAY

JUN

JUL

AUG

SEP

@jamiefahey1 Jamie Fahey
Tragic stories out of Australia but spare a thought for the shockingly under-reported 114 dead in similar floods in Rio #flood #brisbane
12 Jan

In fact, the casualties caused by floods and mudslides in the Brazilian state of Rio de Janeiro would be much higher: over 900 deaths were ultimately reported.

@SultanAlQassemi Sultan Al Qassemi
BBC Breaking news: Tunisia dictator Ben Ali 'will not seek new term' http://bbc.in/e8diqE
13 Jan

@HalaGorani Hala Gorani
Official source: #Tunisia's Ben Ali headed to Paris after being forced from power.
14 Jan

@alya1989262 Alyouka
http://on.fb.me/fBoJWT over 16000 of us are taking to the streets on #jan25! join us:
http://on.fb.me/fQosDi #egypt #tunisia #revolution
15 Jan

This is the first recorded use of the hashtag #jan25, which became the Twitter rallying cry for the Egyptian revolution, long after the date itself had passed.

@VirgoBlue VirgoBlue
Yeah, I'm hoping Ricky Gervais doesn't get to come back. His humor is...how do I say this gently...tasteless and crass. #goldenglobes
16 Jan

@BreakingNews Breaking News
Death toll from floods in Australia at 20 after body found in car - CourierMail http://bit.ly/gZQvys
17 Jan

@TheSourceMag The Source Magazine
Breaking News: In Haiti, former dictator "Baby Doc" Duvalier detained and charged. Why did he return? Stay up @thesourcemag.
18 Jan

@bsebti Bassam Sebti
Islamists in #Jordan to hold protest on Friday to protest the economic situation in the country: http://bit.ly/fqphhS
19 Jan

@peoplemag People magazine
Who isn't addicted to this game? RT @mashable: "Angry Birds" To Become an Animated Series - http://on.mash.to/engKni
20 Jan

@AP The Associated Press
Osama Bin Laden has told France to withdraw troops from Afghanistan in exchange for hostages being freed: http://apne.ws/hvIFZN -EC
21 Jan

@colmtobin Colm Tobin
For those of you who missed Brian Cowen's press conference it can be summed up thus: I'm resigning. I'm not resigning. Fianna Fáil is great.
22 Jan

OCT

NOV

DEC

JAN

FEB

MAR

APR

MAY

JUN

JUL

AUG

SEP

OCT

NOV

DEC

JAN

FEB

MAR

APR

MAY

JUN

JUL

AUG

SEP

@SudanTribune_ENG Sudan Tribune
Over 99.95% vote for southern independence in Eastern
Equatoria http://tiny.cc/zfzoe #Sudan #SthSudan #Africa
#SudanRef
23 Jan

@carlbildt Carl Bildt
Horrible terrorist attack in one of the Moscow airports. Our
deepest sympathies with the Russian people.
24 Jan

@salmaeldaly Salma el Daly
Whole of Tahrir square is one massive cloud now with more
than 50 tear gas cannons fired. #Jan25 #Egypt
25 Jan

@jaidaarab Jaida Arab
Twitter-ban in Egypt won't stop the revolution ...
26 Jan

@Ghonim Wael Ghonim
Pray for #Egypt. Very worried as it seems that
government is planning a war crime tomorrow
against people. We are all ready to die #Jan25
27 Jan

@Omar_Gaza Omar Gaza
Tahrir sq. is now controlled by the protesters! Riot police is on
the roofs shooting bullets and tear-gas grenades!
28 Jan

@richardroeper Richard Roeper
Lindsay Lohan says she's worried about Charlie Sheen. In
other news, a car crash just expressed concerned about a train
wreck.
29 Jan

@SaeedCNN Saeed Ahmed
African Union to form panel of heads of state to resolve the
Ivory Coast crisis: http://on.cnn.com/emlKk0
30 Jan

With the incumbent president Laurent Gbagbo still
refusing to cede power after losing the election in
November, fears were growing that the West African
country could descend into civil war.

@pitchforkmedia Pitchfork
R.I.P. film composer John Barry, man behind the music for
James Bond films, Midnight Cowboy, Dances With Wolves,
more http://bit.ly/hZvMKO
31 Jan

@IranNewsNow Iran News Now
Chant in Tahrir Square: "We are not leaving Thursday - We are
not leaving Friday - We are not leaving!" #Egypt #Jan25
1 Feb

@nolanjourno Dan Nolan
So many bloodied faces pouring out of this battle. Just saw v
young maybe 8yr? old boy unconscious being carried on man's
back #Egypt
2 Feb

@Selintellect Selin.
Gunshots in Tahrir Square NOW, near Qasr al-Nil bridge,
unconfirmed whether army shooting in air, or pro-mubarak
thugs #jan25 #Egypt
3 Feb

OCT
NOV
DEC
JAN
FEB
MAR
APR
MAY
JUN
JUL
AUG
SEP

@Sandmonkey Mahmoud Salem
When this is over, Tahrir square will be the reason tourists will come to Egypt from now on. #jan25
4 Feb

@tarekshalaby Tarek Shalaby
The entire world and half of Egypt is behind us. The remaining will follow when we bring them the revolution. Viva la revolución! #Jan25
5 Feb

@Andre_p_Griffin Andre Griffin
I have to choose between The Steelers and The Packers? This is like a really strange gay porn film plot. #superbowl
6 Feb

@Monasosh Mona Seif
Finally left tahrir square, warm drinks and medicines. We can't let the flue defeat the revolution #Jan25
7 Feb

@IvanCNN Ivan Watson
The crowd in Tahrir Square is HUGE today. More people than I've ever seen. Full from the north end all the way to the Egyptian Museum #Egypt
8 Feb

@MattBinder Matt Binder
GET THE WOMAN SOME TOAST. RT @BreakingNews Update on Gabrielle Giffords' recovery: eating; has made enough speech progress to ask for toast
9 Feb

@monaeltahawy Mona Eltahawy
Civilian-ruled #Egypt is KEY but it looks like our Berlin Wall - #Mubarak - is about to fall. Yalla, Egypt! #Jan25
10 Feb

OCT
NOV
DEC
JAN
FEB
MAR
APR
MAY
JUN
JUL
AUG
SEP

@Amiralx Amira Salah-Ahmed

THIS is the most important moment we have ever experienced...we just ousted a dictator!

#egypt

11 Feb

@Monasosh Mona Seif

Sun is shining on Tahrir square,everyone here is smiling and cleaning. Beautiful people of my country #Jan25

12 Feb

@wossy jonathan ross

Thoroughly enjoyed hosting the Baftas. Best joke- I praised Sir Christopher Lee on his incredible career. He replied " incredible Queer?"

13 Feb

@WSJ Wall Street Journal

Mubarak's resignation in Egypt has emboldened protestors in Iran, Libya, Algeria, Yemen and Bahrain http://on.wsj.com/g9CH9l

14 Feb

@Cyrenaican ساين بنغازي

#libya #feb17 Benghazi calling on everyone to come protest in the streets! Power in numbers! @AJEnglish @AJELive

15 Feb

@camanpour Christiane Amanpour

BBC reports in #Bahrain: tens of thousands are gathered in Pearl Square, Manama. Perhaps biggest crowd yet in this 3-day-old protest.

16 Feb

OCT
NOV
DEC
JAN
FEB
MAR
APR
MAY
JUN
JUL
AUG
SEP

@BBCBreaking BBC Breaking News
BBC Correspondent at Salmaniya Hospital in Manama #Bahrain confirms 3 dead and 300 injured following clashes with police
17 Feb

@Libyan4life Jeel Ghathub
CONFIRMED: INTERNET IS CUT IN ALL OF #LIBYA. Only landlines are working.
18 Feb

@ajc AJC
The End TImes are Upon Us: Bieber is MVP of NBA celebrity game. http://bit.ly/fted3C
19 Feb

@AliDahmash Under My Olive Tree
#Gaddafi son (Saif el eslam) on TV is so boring! Can we skip the interview to pictures of Gaddafi plane leaving Tripoli #Libya
20 Feb

@BreakingNews Breaking News
Libyan justice minister resigns in protest at 'excessive use of violence against protesters,' Quryna newspaper says - Reuters
21 Feb

@miafreedman Mia Freedman
Dark, raining and 13 degrees. Around 200 still trapped and missing under rubble. Thinking of you Christchurch...... xxxx #eqnz #nzeq
22 Feb

@Lord_Voldemort7 The Dark Lord
Lohan meets with a judge today. There's really no need for a judge & trial. Lohan is trying & I judge her. Throw her in Azkaban.
23 Feb

@acarvin Andy Carvin
CNN: protesters have liberated Misrata, Libya's third largest city.
24 Feb

@JessC_M Jess Cartner-Morley
whaaat? RT @BBCBreaking British fashion designer John Galliano arrested in Paris for alleged assault and alleged anti-semitic remarks - AFP
25 Feb

@Libyan4life Jeel Ghathub

TUNISIA --->   : 100% done
EGYPT --->   : 100% done ...
LIBYA --->   : 92% in progress
26 Feb

@ConanOBrien Conan O'Brien
Watching the Oscars. Not crazy about the womb Natalie Portman's baby chose to wear.
27 Feb

@Refugees UN Refugee Agency
#UNHCR erecting tents 4 up 2 10,000 on Tunisia's Libya border. UNHCR staf say area 'saturated', urgent need 2 repatriate thousands Egyptians
28 Feb

@joshuagates Josh Gates
Just watched Charlie Sheen say that he has "tiger's blood" and the "DNA of Adonis." Just so I'm clear...Charlie Sheen is a Thundercat?
1 Mar

@SkyNews Sky News
Libya: Arab Countries Threaten No-Fly Zone http://bit.ly/eYbFTF
2 Mar

NOV
DEC
JAN
FEB
MAR
APR
MAY
JUN
JUL
AUG
SEP

OCT

NOV

DEC

JAN

FEB

MAR

APR

MAY

JUN

JUL

AUG

SEP

@KimberlyHalkett Kimberly Halkett
#Obama: #Gaddafi needs to step down and leave for the good of his country #Libya #breaking
3 Mar

@BinkleyOnStyle Christina Binkley
#Dior got an ovation for bringing out white-coated "petites mains" who worked on the collection. Reminding us that dior isn't galliano.
4 Mar

@fieldproducer Neal Mann
Sky News Correspondent Alex Crawford, who's on the ground in #Zawiyah, reports a column of army tanks moving in to the central Square #Libya
5 Mar

@asa_wire Asa Winstanley
Hilarious: volunteer Libyan fighters have captured "elite" british soldiers: UK papers were full of jingoistic SAS propaganda. #Feb17 #Libya
6 Mar

@EvanHD Evan Davis
Papers full of Prince Andrew. Pressure mounting rather than easing. The Times wants him to go (from his role as trade envoy that is)
7 Mar

The Queen's second son found himself under fire amidst revelations that he had links to Gaddafi's regime and a convicted sex offender, was photographed with an alleged teenaged prostitute, and hosted the son-in-law of the Tunisian dictator, Ben Ali, shortly before he was ousted.

236

OCT
NOV
DEC
JAN
FEB
MAR
APR
MAY
JUN
JUL
AUG
SEP

@RealRobMugabe Robert Mugabe
Our Women's Minister just made a moving speech on
International Women's Day. I texted her, "Good job, love."
#internationalwomendsday
8 Mar

@africamedia_CPJ africamedia_cpj
fearing #egypt style protests, #Cameroon bans mobile
#Twitter service http://bit.ly/gjl1iT #ForeignPolicy #censorship
#socialmedia
9 Mar

@Drudge_Report Drudge Report
Stocks dive on report that Saudis fire on protesters...
http://drudge.tw/dRUh1s
10 Mar

@TomokoHosaka Tomoko A. Hosaka
*Omg. I'm watching NHK footage now of
buildings being washed away in Sendai.*
11 Mar

@kenmogi Ken Mogi
Breaking news. Fuel rod exposed above cooling
water level at Fukushima Nuclear Plant. #earthquake #japan
NHK TV.
12 Mar

@jack Jack Dorsey
5 years ago today we started programming Twitter
("twttr" for short). 8 days later the first tweet was sent:
j.mp/19bhrr #twttr
13 Mar

OCT

NOV

DEC

JAN

FEB

MAR

APR

MAY

JUN

JUL

AUG

SEP

@TimeOutTokyo TimeOutTokyo
A choir of pre-quake alarms! @jt_sloosh: In a packed train and everyone's quake alarms went off at once. THAT'S SCARY! #japanquake
14 Mar

@BlackNerd Andre Black Nerd
Rebecca Black "Friday" gets over 2.2 million views over the weekend. That's it. I quit. http://yhoo.it/fPvj9L
15 Mar

Despite a devastating earthquake in Japan and domino-effect political unrest in the Middle East, one of the top trending topics on Twitter this week was Rebecca Black, a 13-year-old wannabe popstar, whose song 'Friday' contained such lyrical gems as, 'Kickin' in the front seat/Sittin' in the back seat/Gotta make my mind up/Which seat can I take?'

@andersoncooper Anderson Cooper
Shocking video out of #bahrain, man shot point blank by authorities. #ac360 10p
16 Mar

@msnbc_business msnbc.com - Business
Bahrain tensions drive oil prices up again
http://on.msnbc.com/fDAYUt
17 Mar

@monaeltahawy Mona Eltahawy
So in #Saudi Arabia today, King Abdullah's message not Power to the People but Money to the People? Did I get that right?!
18 Mar

OCT

NOV

DEC

JAN

FEB

MAR

APR

MAY

JUN

JUL

AUG

SEP

@Ghonim Wael Ghonim
Egyptians waiting in lines in front of a polling station in Nasr
City in Cairo one hour before the station opens :
http://twitpic.com/4axn0v
19 Mar

@NASA NASA
It's the Supermoon! Look what @nasahqphoto captured: The
perigee super moon of 2011 rises behind the Lincoln Memorial
flic.kr/p/9rDmc6
20 Mar

@SultanAlQassemi Sultan Al Qassemi
Every dictator in the Arab world thinks that he is not a dictator.
21 Mar

@DRUNKHULK DRUNK HULK
WOW! DRUNK HULK DISCOVER PARADOX! KICK IN FRONT
SEAT! SIT IN BACK SEAT! GOT MAKE MIND UP! WHICH SEAT
CAN DRUNK HULK TAKE!
22 Mar

@TweetOfSatan Lucifer
#thatwasawkward lighting a nice big fire for Colonel Gaddafi
then being told he's not actually dead yet.
23 Mar

@ActuallyNPH Neil Patrick Harris
Harry Houdini was born on this day,
137 years ago. When using handcuffs or other
restraints tonight, please do so in his honor.
24 Mar

@TopJournalism Jean-Fancois Huerta
The west is not taking sides in Libya, it is making up for having
favoured one side for decades #Libyan #no-fly
25 Mar

OCT
NOV
DEC
JAN
FEB
MAR
APR
MAY
JUN
JUL
AUG
SEP

@jeremyscahill jeremy scahill
President Saleh will step down as soon as he finishes not
stepping down. #Yemen
26 Mar

@SultanAlQassemi Sultan Al Qassemi
Maher Al Assad, brother of Syrian dictator enjoys filming
massacred Syrian protesters http://bit.ly/dXN8O4 Extremely
Graphic Video 1:17m
27 Mar

@BronxZoosCobra Bronx Zoo's Cobra
Donald Trump is thinking about running for president?! Don't
worry, I'll handle this. Where is Trump Tower exactly?
28 Mar

@calperryAJ Cal Perry

*We can now safely say there are hundreds
of thousands of people on the streets of
#damascus: and it's still getting bigger.* #syria
29 Mar

@foreignoffice Foreign Office (FCO)
#Libya: Foreign Office spokesperson confirms Musa Kusa
arrived at Farnborough Airport on 30 March from Tunisia.
http://ow.ly/4pTai
30 Mar

@ragehomaar Rageh Omaar
and so it begins in syria. nmbr of emails from friends in syria
with differing viewpoints but all thnk assad speech yday
turning point
31 Mar

@Tharwacolamus Ammar Abdulhamid
#Homs #Syria: 6 martyrs, 65 wounded, 64 arrested, so far, protests in many neighborhoods continue, rest of city ghost town #March15 #Assad
1 Apr

@ReThinkOrg ReThinkTank
9 die in #Kandahar as protests spread over Florida pastor's burning of a #Koran last month. Taliban attack NATO compound: http://ow.ly/4rOZV
2 Apr

@melissakchan Melissa Chan
China's best-known artist, Ai Wei Wei, designer of Olympic stadium, detained. Studio surrounded by police.
3 Apr

@RAGreeneCNN RAGreeneCNN
Breaking: At least 11 dead, 500 injured in demonstration in #Taiz #Yemen, medical sources there tell CNN
4 Apr

@CBSNews CBS News
UN, French troops poised to remove Ivory Coast strongman Laurent Gbagbo from power, by force: http://bit.ly/g4ePTn
5 Apr

@BarbaraGSerra Barbara Serra
At #berlusconi #Bungabunga trial. No silvio or girls attending, but world's TVs here, all talking about sex parties in various languages
6 Apr

OCT
NOV
DEC
JAN
FEB
MAR
APR
MAY
JUN
JUL
AUG
SEP

@GlobalGrind Global Grind
#Tsunami warning lifted in Japan after 7.4 earthquake hit Japan.
7 Apr

@UNrightswire UN Human Rights
UN Human Rights teams found over a hundred bodies in western #Côte d'Ivoire yesterday - http://goo.gl/9DBKp #humanrights
8 Apr

@Drudge_Report Drudge Report
UPDATE: Ivory Coast mercenaries 'are burning people alive'... http://drudge.tw/eHvlL4
9 Apr

@GuardianUSA GuardianUSA
Evidence grows of Ivory Coast atrocities by Ouattara and Gbagbo supporters http://gu.com/p/2zbjp/tf
10 Apr

@UN United Nations
Côte d'Ivoire: #UN peacekeeping mission confirms that Gbagbo has surrendered to forces loyal to elected president http://bit.ly/hVruLW
11 Apr

@Jkchavanne Julie Kaye
Wonder what Rod thinks! RT @OKMagazine Benicio Del Toro & Kim Stewart Expecting First Child Together, Not Dating http://bit.ly/fke5mx
12 Apr

@ericasfish Erica's Fish
Why can't I have a single conversation with this cat without her stopping to lick her own butt.
13 Apr

OCT

NOV

DEC

JAN

FEB

MAR

APR

MAY

JUN

JUL

AUG

SEP

@jellison22 jo ellison
Closer and closer... RT @arusbridger: Here's the story on the
latest phone-hacking arrest http://bit.ly/hEQals #coulson
#metgate
14 Apr

@rallaf Rime
Something's changed! #Aljazeera Arabic showing #Syria
protests in a loop, city after city, without comments, letting us
hear strong slogans!
15 Apr

@DannySeesIt Daniel
"The new cabinet is new hopes for the citizens" - Bashar Al-
Assad speech. #syria
16 Apr

@tweetminster Tweetminster
*"#Syria secret police tell parents of arrested
protesters to forget their children and have
some more"* http://bit.ly/gCZTWB - Mail Online
17 Apr

@arwaCNN Arwa Damon
On Sat #syria president promised reforms & lifting of
emergency law w/in week, on Sun reports of clashes & more
deaths.
18 Apr

@foreignoffice Foreign Office (FCO)
Foreign Secretary @WilliamJHague announces the expansion
of the #UK diplomatic team in Benghazi http://ow.ly/4Dhgh
#Libya
19 Apr

OCT
NOV
DEC
JAN
FEB
MAR
APR
MAY
JUN
JUL
AUG
SEP

@HuffingtonPost Huffington Post
Oscar-nominated journalist Tim Hetherington, photographer
Chris Hondros reportedly killed in Libya http://huff.to/fjLjkq
20 Apr

@cshirky Clay Shirky
Bahrain Govt detains doctors who treat protestors
http://ind.pn/gyjotT These are US allies; where are Obama
or Clinton on this?
21 Apr

@NewsFromAmnesty Amnesty UK media
At least 75 killed in #Syria as 'Great Friday' protests attacked
http://bit.ly/gS4Kfr
22 Apr

@ed_vincent Edward Vincent
Good to see the Royal Family showing solidarity with the
tyrannts of Bahrain by inviting them to the wedding...#Bahrain
23 Apr

@Srinjoy Srinjoy Sen
Syria: 120 dead after two days of unrest: Two lawmakers and a
religious leader resigned in disgust over the killings. http://bit.
ly/e1feGP
24 Apr

@AlOraibi Mina Al-Oraibi
No surprises in @wikileaks Guantanamo Bay documents,
innocents held, years uncharged, but their publication is
important for the record
25 Apr

@GovBeebeMedia Matt DeCample
Governor Beebe has declared a statewide State of Emergency
in response to the tornadoes and flooding. #ARWX
26 Apr

OCT

NOV

DEC

JAN

FEB

MAR

APR

MAY

JUN

JUL

AUG

SEP

@andytwood Andy Wood
Newly released long-form bith certificate deemed "too long"--birthers call for Obama to release his medium-length one. #justright
27 Apr

@twister_tracker Twister Tracker
What an insane day. We've logged 427 #tornado warnings issued today and we're not done yet.
http://www.twistertracker.com #alwx #tnwx #mswx
28 Apr

@richardpbacon richard bacon
The Royal Wedding drinking game begins now. Down a shot every time a broadcaster says "extraordinary scenes" and "sea of flags".
29 Apr

@SultanAlQassemi Sultan Al Qassemi
Breaking BBC Arabic: One of Gaddafi's sons and three of his grandchildren have been killed in a NATO strike. #Libya
30 Apr

@DianaInHeaven Princess Diana
Pope John Paul II has been on the lash most of the day since being beatified. I'm not holding the fucker's hair back when he starts puking.
1 May

@graceisabel Grace Fernandez
A Royal wedding, Pope John Paul II was beatified, Osama Bin Laden Dead. #whataweek
2 May

OCT

NOV

DEC

JAN

FEB

MAR

APR

MAY

JUN

JUL

AUG

SEP

@SkyNewsPolitics SkyNewsPolitics
Mudslinging Continues As Elections Draw Near: Sniping over
the alternative vote referendum has stepped up a gear...
http://bit.ly/mmndSO
3 May

@TwopTwips Twop Twips
SHOW your wife that you understand 'AV' by telling her she's
your no.1 then shagging her sister. /via @ScurrilousFacts
4 May

@ns_mehdihasan Mehdi Hasan
According to YouGov "exit poll", one in five Lib Dems (Lib
Dems!) voted No to #AV. Pretty much sums up the problems
faced by Yes campaign
5 May

@itn ITN
*Blow for #NickClegg and the Lib Dems after
#AV referendum defeat.* (http://bit.ly/lbDU8I)
6 May

@FrankRGardner Frank Gardner
First apparent retaliation for #OBL death - Afgh Taliban bomb
govt targets in Kandahar killing 2.
7 May

@PostWorldNews Post World News
Italian police save 400 migrants after boat crashes against
rocks at Lampedusa port http://wapo.st/l6RFXN
8 May

@VantageNews Vantage News
Nato units left 61 African migrants to die of hunger and thirst
gu.com/p/2pvc7/tw #Lampedusa #NATO #EU
9 May

@jellison22 jo ellison
Everyone in my tube carriage reading evening standard is reading spread on Pippa Middleton. Old, young, black, white, male, female. All
10 May

@newtgingrich Newt Gingrich
Today I am announcing my candidacy for President of the United States. You can watch my announcement here. http://bit.ly/kEbh7d
11 May

@LoreleiKing Lorelei King
Princess Beatrice to auction 'that hat' on eBay. Don't all rush. http://tinyurl.com/69ghkhh
12 May

@SiClancy Simon Clancy
Gruesome story on the BBC News site: "A British woman has been beheaded in a shop in Spain's Canary Islands, officials say."
13 May

@Queen_UK Elizabeth Windsor
RAF stand by. #eurovision
14 May

@PatateVertigo Jey

Shocking Sex Assault Arrest of IMF Chief Dominique Strauss-Kahn Throws French Presidential Race Into Chaos

http://ti.me/mxtl7v #Time #News
15 May

@JimBarrowman James Barrowman
Dominique Strauss-Khan is apparently seeking a super injunction to prevent the media accusing him of being a banker.
16 May

OCT

NOV

DEC

JAN

FEB

MAR

APR

MAY

JUN

JUL

AUG

SEP

OCT
NOV
DEC
JAN
FEB
MAR
APR
MAY
JUN
JUL
AUG
SEP

@GeorgeTakei George Takei
Schwarzenegger confesses to fathering baby with house staff member, but explains that child is destined to bring down SkyNet in 2031.
17 May

@TVGuide TV Guide
VIDEO: Director Lars von Trier says he's a Nazi and sympathizes with Hitler at Cannes Film Festival http://bit.ly/j2bZD4
18 May

@paulocoelho Paulo Coelho
Epidemy of pathetic remarks. Lars Von Trier in Cannes: "I understand Hitler[...]. I sympathise with him" #notfunny
19 May

@HoeZaay José Covaco
Dominique Strauss-Kahn steps down as IMF as they repeatedly rejected his proposal to change the name to MILF.
20 May

@DavidCampbell73 David Campbell
Dammit. Still here. #rapture #fail
21 May

@RyanJL Ryan Love
So that's, 'ITV2s BAFTA-Award winning The Only Way Is Essex' from now on then. And we all thought #Rapture was yesterday. #baftas
22 May

@CBSNews CBS News
BREAKING: Authorities say at least 89 killed by massive tornado in Missouri
23 May

@funnyhumour funny humour
Ryan Giggs today admitted to suffering from homesickness, saying that even though he's happy in Manchester he does Miss Wales occasionally.
24 May

@usweekly Us Weekly
She's a trendsetter! The $340 Reiss dress Kate Middleton wore to meet the Obamas is already sold-out! http://goo.gl/JuIp6
25 May

@AnnCurry Ann Curry
ARRESTED: Ratko Mladic wanted for genocide of 8,000 Bosnian muslims between 1992-95. You can't hide forever.
26 May

@PayneKate kate payne
I don't recall Twitter asking me if I'd like to receive email every time I get an @ reply. Like I need more superfluous email...
27 May

@missrachilli Rachel Shillcock
GET IN!!! come on united!!! Great goal from Rooney there! #championsleaguefinal
28 May

@Liberationtech Liberationtech
13-year-old boy tortured to death - Hamza Ali Al Khateeb - becomes symbol of Syria uprising http://is.gd/SZIWKJ
29 May

@heyessa Essa
Malta says yes to #divorce; #Philippines & Vatican City the last 2 states where it remains illegal | http://bit.ly/lAf9Yi | via @AJEnglish
30 May

OCT
NOV
DEC
JAN
FEB
MAR
APR
MAY
JUN
JUL
AUG
SEP

OCT

NOV

DEC

JAN

FEB

MAR

APR

MAY

JUN

JUL

AUG

SEP

@ Nora_LUMIERE Nora Lumiere
Only male maids for Dominique Strauss-Kahn at the NY apartment where he's under house arrest http://bit.ly/iCX9ST #DSK
31 May

@ryanhanrahan Ryan Hanrahan
I can't express the seriousness of the storm heading toward Sturbridge just south of Mass Pike near 84. Tornado ON THE GROUND
1 Jun

@badbanana Tim Siedell
For now, I'm avoiding vegetables because of this e-coli scare. Eventually I'll go back to not eating them for other reasons.
2 Jun

@funnyordie Funny Or Die
Let's use Jack Kevorkian's death as an opportunity to ponder our own mortali- wait, it's #nationaldonutday?!? FREE DONUTS, you guys!!!
3 Jun

@MrsStephenFry Mrs Stephen Fry
EXCLUSIVE: First Wayne Rooney hair transplant picture released. #hairwego http://twitpic.com/56uzh4
4 Jun

@marytwocats mary wycherley
Oh man I've knackered the couch with amniotic fluid.
5 Jun

@Caissie Caissie St.Onge
Are we still allowed to like Anthony Weiner? Name one other politician who's been indiscreet so efficiently & cheaply.
6 Jun

@friedmanjon Jon Friedman
Now that he's apologized, Anthony Weiner can move on and feel lucky that there's nothing about this that will serve as a constant reminder.
7 Jun

@RexHuppke Rex Huppke
If it's a boy, the Weiners will name their first child John Thomas.
8 Jun

@BrennanLA Andrew Brennan
Two new elements on the Periodic Table need names. Waiting for somebody to suggest kardashium.
9 Jun

@DianaInHeaven Princess Diana
He'd have preferred a blowjob RT @SkyNewsBreak Queen conferrs title & office of Lord High Admiral to Duke of Edinburgh on his 90th birthday
10 Jun

@BillMc7 Bill Mc7
I've sent pictures of my wiener to dozens of women on Twitter, and I can't get the news media to even give me an honorable mention!
11 Jun

@JoshMalina Joshua Malina
Programming the NBA finals opposite the Tony Awards is unfair to dozens of people worldwide.
12 Jun

OCT
NOV
DEC
JAN
FEB
MAR
APR
MAY
JUN
JUL
AUG
SEP

OCT

NOV

DEC

JAN

FEB

MAR

APR

MAY

JUN

JUL

AUG

SEP

@laurennmcc Laurenn McCubbin
I respect his decision, but devastated that we'll be losing him.
Terry Pratchett petitions for assisted suicide:
http://tinyurl.com/6y8jf58
13 Jun

@AngryBritain AngryBritain.com
I don't know what the big deal is about the one-off Terry
Pratchett show. #xfactor encourages suicide for
12 whole weeks.
14 Jun

@DeathStarPR Death Star PR
Natalie Portman had a son. In unrelated news, everyone
here on the Death Star is suddenly looking a little nervous.
#StarWars
15 Jun

@TheEllenShow Ellen DeGeneres
*Great news in NY. Their state assembly
approved a marriage equality bill and it's
off to the senate! It's up to you, NY!*
16 Jun

@Women2Drive Women
Yes, we drove. #Women2Drive
17 Jun

Inspired by the revolutions traversing the Arab world,
women in ultra-conservative Saudi Arabia convened on
social media, defied the religious fatwa and got behind
the wheel. In September, they won the right to vote.

@thelittleidiot moby

Playing a festival in serbia with amy winehouse and she's on stage mumbling... ah boy, can't someone do an intervention? Its heartbreaking.

18 Jun

@JamesPMorrison James Morrison
Rory McIlvoy, 22-years-old from Northern Ireland, wins US Open. Record 16 under. Bam! Thank you!
19 Jun

@simonpegg Simon Pegg
Goodnight all. Sad news about Ryan Dunn, have always loved Jackass. He was a credit to craziness. Thoughts are with his friends and family.
20 Jun

@TweetChina Tweet China
Death toll reaches 175 in south China flooding since early June http://bit.ly/kqjeZD #china
21 Jun

@diamondgeezer diamond geezer
Ooh, ooh, no need to wait for the official email... Look, I got Olympic tickets! For, ooh, that. And, blimey, that. And... ooh.
22 Jun

@funnyordie Funny Or Die
Good news, ladies! George Clooney is single again! Bad news: it's a male dominated world w/ systematic oppression & also you menstruate.
23 Jun

OCT

NOV

DEC

JAN

FEB

MAR

APR

MAY

JUN

JUL

AUG

SEP

@ActuallyNPH Neil Patrick Harris
It PASSED! Marriage equality in NY!! Yes!! Progress!! Thank
you everyone who worked so hard on this!!
A historic night!
24 Jun

@JarettSays Jarett Wieselman
WHAT!?!?!? RT @ETonlineAlert: Congrats to Daniel Craig,
reportedly married Rachel Weisz in a secret ceremony! http://
etonline.com/p/?8p93zt
25 Jun

@CherylKerl Cheryl Kerl
#Beyonce man, meind oot man aw yerz meight stawt a riot
wur thim gyrashinz. Yerz mebbes shudda wawn a pettikert pet
#Glasto
26 Jun

@Slate Slate
Michele Bachmann officially announces her candidacy,
reminding everyone 'I'm from Iowa': http://slate.me/kgnTAw
27 Jun

@darthvader Darth Vader
I hate days when I wake up on the right side of the bed.
28 Jun

@markknoller Mark Knoller
Pres Obama said Congress passed the bills and spent the
money and has to act responsibly and "do the job" by raising
the debt limit.
29 Jun

@tech2learn Randall Dennis
Now THIS is hilarious: MI6 hacks terrorists, replaces bomb
instructions with cupcakes recipes - http://ow.ly/5tW59
http://ow.ly/1udi6D
30 Jun

OCT

NOV

DEC

JAN

FEB

MAR

APR

MAY

JUN

JUL

AUG

SEP

@suntimesbazzaf Barry Flatman
Big day for @andy_murray today. Could be one to really remember
1 Jul

@richardquest Richard Quest
Civil wedding was yesterday...today is religious ceremony. ...always love monaco
2 Jul

@fuggirls Go Fug Yourself
Doing a little work before getting my BBQ on. Dude, NO ONE at the Royal Wedding in Monaco looks happy. - J
3 Jul

@Sai__kun Carlos Revollo
personally, i won't believe #obamadead until i see a death certificate.
4 Jul

@bnu Breaking News Update
[680News] Florida woman Casey Anthony has been found not guilty of first-degree murder of her two-year-old daughter...
http://is.gd/FafzKK
5 Jul

@ohsouthlondon Ben
Just seen a guy with a sandwich board that read "THE END OF THE NEWS OF THE WORLD IS NIGH".
6 Jul

@Ed_Miliband Ed Miliband
The one person who seems to have kept her job was Editor when Milly Dowler's phone was hacked and is in charge of News International.
7 Jul

OCT

NOV

DEC

JAN

FEB

MAR

APR

MAY

JUN

JUL

AUG

SEP

@Aiannucci Armando Iannucci
Ok, Twitter, can we deal with the Horn of Africa next?
8 Jul

@grahamsalisbury Graham Salisbury
Dig Deep! Don't leave it up to others to contribute to
@decappeal to help those affected by the worst drought in
60 years in East Africa
9 Jul

@andrewwander Andrew Wander
Elderly man, terribly emaciated, sitting in the dirt begging me
for help. Never felt so powerless in my life #dadaab #eastafrica
10 Jul

@Tzarimas Helen Tzarimas
Guys, there is such severe famine in the Horn of Africa, that it's
threatening the lives of 10 MILLION PEOPLE.....
http://bit.ly/orrM7F
11 Jul

@Oxfam Oxfam International
#Kenya refuses to open empty #refugee camp as thousands
flee famine http://tgr.ph/nDIFcV #drought #humanitarian
12 Jul

@maddow Rachel Maddow MSNBC
Grief-stricken Hamid Karzai climbs into brother's grave:
is.gd/Fa3LTE
13 Jul

@richardpbacon richard bacon
Ricky Gervais' Golden Globes performance has been
nominated for an Emmy. Some reporters the following day
claimed he'd "never work again".
14 Jul

OCT

NOV

DEC

JAN

FEB

MAR

APR

MAY

JUN

JUL

AUG

SEP

@fuggirls Go Fug Yourself
I go out of town for the weekend and J Lo and Marc Anthony
BREAK UP!?! ADIOS LOVERS?!!? - J
15 Jul

@Astro_Satoshi 古川聡（ＪＡＸＡ宇宙飛行士）
Four Space Shuttle and six ISS crew members had the dinner
together at the Space Shuttle. I ate the grilled chicken and the
spinach.
16 Jul

@SteveMartinToGo Steve Martin
I will feel so bad if I'm not one of the celebrities on the hacked
list of the News of the World.
17 Jul

@Bynickdavies Nick Davies
In memory of Sean Hoare, News of the World reporter and
whistleblower who died today. tinyurl.com/6k3m3yz
18 Jul

@KathViner Katharine Viner
Wendi for CEO of News Corp
19 Jul

@mariellaf1 Mariella Frostrup
*Would Murdoch donate £1million to famine
victims whose plight has been kept off front
pages by NI #hackgate. How about it?*
20 Jul

@BorowitzReport Andy Borowitz
BREAKING: GOP Proposes Replacing Social Security with
Letting People Eat Cake
21 Jul

OCT
NOV
DEC
JAN
FEB
MAR
APR
MAY
JUN
JUL
AUG
SEP

@ketilbstensrud Ketil B. Stensrud

A man disguised in a police uniform is, according to live tweets FROM Utøya, shooting 'wildly' at people as people hide behind bushes.

22 Jul

@jo_elvin Jo Elvin
Just landed in London and shocked to read about Amy Winehouse. I think she was one of the sweetest, humblest people I'd ever met.
23 Jul

@Iskwew Iskwew
Police Say Oslo Suspect Admits 'Facts,' not Guilt, in Massacre - http://nyti.ms/pxN0jc
24 Jul

@5STARSUE SUE SMITH
Ha ha ha !!! RT @Gally_7: Off to bed to smash @HayleyGa11agher back doors in ,,
25 Jul

With only his second tweet, Leicester City striker Paul Gallagher (@Gally_7) managed to embarrass his wife (@HayleyGallagher), get retweeted by his apparently unshockable mother (@5STARSUE) and inspire an awful lot of tabloid headlines.

@BuzzFeed BuzzFeed
Happy birthday Dame Helen Mirren. 66-year-old hottie.
26 Jul

@Nouriel Nouriel Roubini
Reagan raised the debt ceiling 18x, Bush 7x by 4 trillion. Now Republicans pretend to be born-again debt virgins when they fed the beast
27 Jul

@ChrisBryantMP Chris Bryant
Utter utter hypocrisy to give Sara Payne a mobile and then have it hacked. 'smile and smile and be a villiain' #hackgate
28 Jul

@TechCrunch TechCrunch
President Obama Calls On U.S. Citizens To 'Tweet' To Lawmakers About Raising Debt Ceiling http://tcrn.ch/nEdWlD by @leenarao
29 Jul

@HowardKurtz HowardKurtz
102 degrees in DC today. If we made all the lawmakers negotiate outside, the debt crisis would be solved in an hour.
30 Jul

@GhostPanther Adam McKay
Using obama's negotiating method with my six year old. She gets 20 gallons of choco syrup, American Girl Doll. I get her not crying.
31 Jul

@pourmecoffee pourmecoffee
As soon as debt deal passes, feral packs of Job Creators will be sprung hungry from their cages to Create Jobs.
1 Aug

@AriMelber Ari Melber
Tired of dropping in response to political theatrics, the stock market now goes back to dropping in response to a weak economy.
2 Aug

OCT

NOV

DEC

JAN

FEB

MAR

APR

MAY

JUN

JUL

AUG

SEP

OCT

NOV

DEC

JAN

FEB

MAR

APR

MAY

JUN

JUL

AUG

SEP

@pwire Taegan Goddard
Former White House adviser Larry Summers says chance of
double-dip recession is now 1 in 3... http://pwire.at/qpLs1A
3 Aug

@LarrySabato Larry Sabato
Suddenly, turning 50 isn't President Obama's worst memory of
Aug. 4, 2011.
4 Aug

Despite the US debt deal, anxieties over the health of
the world economy cause stock markets in Europe and
the US to tumble. The Dow suffers its biggest single-
day loss since the banking crisis of 2008.

@londontonight ITV London Tonight
A man shot dead by police in Tottenham, after an apparent
exchange of fire, was a passenger in a minicab, they said today
5 Aug

@AfghanNews24 AfghanNews
NATO helicopter crashes in Afghanistan, killing 31 U.S. troops
http://ow.ly/1e7OGK
6 Aug

@Paullewis Paul Lewis
Loud bangs now in #tottenhamriot. TV cameras well outside
cordon. Police van arriving pelted with bricks.
7 Aug

@AndrewMaleMojo Andrew Male
I wish the BBC news would stop doing those segues from
"riots" to "global financial meltdown". I feel like I'm in
RoboCop.
8 Aug

@vacuumcleaner the vacuum cleaner
#riotcleanup - a perfect example of anarchy.
9 Aug

@simonpegg Simon Pegg

Love that Kaiser Chiefs were on hand to help out with @Riotcleanup. They could've quite easily sat back and said I told you so.
10 Aug

@DylanJonesGQ Dylan Jones
According to the Mirror, online sales of baseball bats rose by 6,000% yesterday, the suggestion being they are being bought by vigilantes.
11 Aug

@Paullewis Paul Lewis
BREAKING: IPCC has announced it may have "inadvertently" led journalists to believe Mark Duggan shot at police
12 Aug

@HawkinsJT Jack Hawkins
Wandsworth council to evict mother of charged boy gu.com/p/3x7t8/tw - Daily Mail reactionary stupidity, far more dangerous than any riot
13 Aug

@WendytheBee Wendy B
Wow!! London courts are so full of riot suspects, that they are open on Sunday!!! tinyurl.com/3fqp2mg
14 Aug

@PayneKate kate payne
Warren Buffet lays it out in this great @nytimes op-ed piece, "Stop Coddling the Super-Rich": tinyurl.com/3wftfd2
15 Aug

OCT
NOV
DEC
JAN
FEB
MAR
APR
MAY
JUN
JUL
AUG
SEP

@KathViner Katharine Viner
FOUR YEARS RT @PaulLewis Two men each jailed for
4 years for encouraging #riots (which never happened) on
Facebook
16 Aug

@LisaSkyNews Lisa Dowd
Fourth person charged with murders of 3 men who were hit
by car while protecting shops from looters in Birmingham
#riots
17 Aug

@Peston Robert Peston
Hugo Chavez is repatriating 99 tons of Venezuelan gold held
in the Bank of England's vaults. Says he doesn't think it's safe
there. Hmmm
18 Aug

@Number10gov UK Prime Minister
David Cameron condemns the "vicious and cowardly" attack
on the British Council building in #Kabul bit.ly/pLd32i
19 Aug

@sarasidnerCNN Sara Sidner
Just returned from Zawiya, Libya. It appears Rebels have taken
the entire town. Rockets still falling into city but Gadhafi
forces are out.
20 Aug

@mchancecnn Matthew Chance
Govt officials: Eastern suburbs of capital are out government
control and in rebel hands #CNN #Libya #tripoli
21 Aug

@lindseyhilsum Lindsey Hilsum
I asked a man at the side fo the a road "where is Gaddafi" - he
said "gone with the wind" #Libya #Tripoli
22 Aug

@JesseCFriedman Jesse Friedman
I saw the tweets from DC about earthquake, then 15 seconds later felt it in NYC. Social media is faster than seismic waves!
23 Aug

@GarethAveyard Gareth Aveyard
Steve Jobs' text was meant to say: "I reign as CEO of Apple" Damn you autocorrect!
24 Aug

@edyong209 Ed Yong

In Gaddafi's lair, rebels find photo album full of page after page of Condoleeza Rice. AWKWAAARD on.msnbc.com/pvncQxw/ working link
25 Aug

@piersmorgan Piers Morgan
Hurricane #Irene is bigger than EUROPE. And heading straight for NYC. This is getting pretty scary.
26 Aug

@MikeBloomberg Mike Bloomberg
You can't prepare for the best case, you have to prepare for the worst case bit.ly/r2MvC7 #Irene
27 Aug

@Gene_Cowan47 Gene
Dear NYC... please get over yourself... Vermont and Upstate NY are UNDER WATER. #irene
28 Aug

@Slate Slate
CNN tracks down Lockerbie bomber in Libya, finds him "near death." slate.me/raUsAu via @Slatest
29 Aug

OCT

NOV

DEC

JAN

FEB

MAR

APR

MAY

JUN

JUL

AUG

SEP

@MatthewWells Matt Wells
Media is being hammered for overhyping threat to New York and simultaneously underhyping Vermont. Both are true I think. #irene
30 Aug

@swirlywand Staci M.
Are u kidding me??? TX had this ridiculous law??? RT "@cnnbrk: Judge strikes parts of Texas sonogram abortion law. on.cnn.com/qU2u7K
31 Aug

@itn ITN
The end of an era: David Cameron thanks Wootton Bassett as he hands over repatriation duties to RAF Brize Norton...
bit.ly/qdqo16
1 Sep

@KerryParnell Kerry Parnell
Shane Warne alleges media removed his wrinkles in photos. They left in the taut skin, white teeth, alarming eyebrows and hair implants then
2 Sep

@der_bluthund Anonymous Watcher

So both the CIA and MI6 were doing extraordinary renditions to Libya under Gaddafi's Regime? Some days even I have trouble comprehending...

3 Sep

@joshthomas87 Josh thomas
'U by Kotex found out 3 out of 4 of you suffer 'leakage-paranoia' LA LA LA I'M NOT LISTENING LA LA LA
4 Sep

OCT

NOV

DEC

JAN

FEB

MAR

APR

MAY

JUN

JUL

AUG

@Peston Robert Peston
The spread between Italian and German gov bond yields nears record again. Means euro sovereign debt crisis flaring up again, with vengeance
5 Sep

@fuggirls Go Fug Yourself
I can't believe Eddie Murphy is hosting the Oscars. Have we all tripped and fallen into 1984? - J
6 Sep

@MarjorieBelles Marjorie Belles
Having to tear myself away from the bbc bar #strictly mania has arrived.I saw #rorybremner and #anitadobson.Can't wait for it to start
7 Sep

@markknoller Mark Knoller
In speech tonight, Pres Obama will ask Congress whether "we can stop the political circus and actually do something to help the economy."
8 Sep

@WSJ Wall Street Journal
Here's the latest on the "credible" threat of car or truck bombings in Washington and New York City:
on.wsj.com/nRUj8F
9 Sep

@michellemalkin Michelle Malkin
Remembrance is worthless without resolve. Resolve is useless without action. #911
10 Sep

OCT

NOV

DEC

JAN

FEB

MAR

APR

MAY

JUN

JUL

AUG

SEP

@mrjoezee Joe Zee

I get up, get dressed & head to work today, exactly as I did 10 yrs ago, but that day changed our country & our lives forever. Never Forget.

11 Sep

@jonsnowC4 Jon Snow
Semi naked men welcome David Walliams at the end of his desperate £1m charity fund raiser in the Thames..great achievement..the swim I mean!
12 Sep

@LIFE LIFE.com
Well, that's an unlikely pair? — Nicki Minaj & Anna Wintour at Fashion Week: on.life.com/qtaDgl I pic.twitter.com/WDGJkzW
13 Sep

@jayrosen_nyu Jay Rosen
The AP has called the race to replace Anthony Weiner for the Republican. In reply, Obama is preparing some bold new pre-emptive compromises.
14 Sep

@aliceemross Alice Ross
The final facebook update of Kweku Adoboli at UBS was: "Need a miracle." #UBS #roguetrader
15 Sep

@ahmed Ahmed Al Omran
Heartbreaking: mother washing her son who was shot dead in Idlib today. "He doesn't like hot water," she says bit.ly/oO1HWC #syria
16 Sep

@guardianeco Guardian Environment
Welsh miners' families face their loss after hopes of rescue are dashed gu.com/p/32xhk/tf
17 Sep

@JoshMalina Joshua Malina
Huzzah for Downton Abbey! #Emmys
18 Sep

@DougSaunders Doug Saunders
I'm not tweeting the images out of Yemen today. There are limits. Suffice to say it was clearly a mass atrocity of unforgivable magnitude.
19 Sep

@whitehouse The White House
As of 12:01 am, the repeal of the discriminatory law known as 'Don't Ask, Don't Tell' finally & formally takes effect. #DADT
20 Sep

OCT
NOV
DEC
JAN
FEB
MAR
APR
MAY
JUN
JUL
AUG
SEP

INTRO

POLITICS &
CURRENT AFFAIRS

ROYALTY &
RELIGION

CELEBRITY

SCIENCE &
NATURE

SPORT &
LEISURE

ARTS, CULTURE
& MEDIA

A TWEET A DAY

GLOSSARY
& THANKS

— Glossary —

Below are the most common terms you'll come across when talking about Twitter or looking at the website. Note that these all refer specifically to the website itself, not to interfaces such as Tweetdeck or Hootsuite.

@ The symbol used to facilitate conversation between users. When a username is preceded immediately by @, it becomes a link to their profile page, and it also makes your tweet appear in the mentions section on their home page, even if they don't follow you. You can either simply type it in (this is known as an '@mention'), or click Reply and it will automatically appear at the beginning of your tweet (this is known as an '@reply'). Both types appear in the mentions or @[username] section; a speech bubble symbol denotes @replies.

@Mention *See @.*

@Reply *See @.*

* Asterisk, often put on either side of something as a type of parenthesis. Frequently used for comedic effect, or to indicate a sound or movement, e.g. *shuffles papers*, or *looks at watch*.

*See Hashtags.*

Activity A section of your homepage that allows you to see what your followers have been up to.

Block To stop someone following you or to avoid seeing when they mention you. You can do this by going to their profile page, clicking on the Person symbol and choosing the option 'Block'.

INTRO

POLITICS &
CURRENT AFFAIRS

ROYALTY &
RELIGION

CELEBRITY

SCIENCE &
NATURE

SPORT &
LEISURE

ARTS, CULTURE
& MEDIA

A TWEET A DAY

GLOSSARY
& THANKS

Direct message (DM) Private messages that can be sent between users.

Emoticons Punctuation symbols used to make pictures, usually faces, that are visible when you tilt your head to one side.

Fail whale Nickname for the cartoon that appears when the site is overloaded.

Favourite A link that lets you save a tweet in your favourites list. You can access this list from your profile page.

Feed The tweets posted by any one Twitter user.

#FF Follow Friday, when users often recommend other users to their followers. Sometimes also written out as #followfriday.

FFS For fuck's sake.

Follow As a verb, to opt to see a particular user's tweets in your home timeline. As a noun, it is sometimes used to mean the act of following, as in, 'Can I have a follow?'

Followers The people who are following you. This number on your home page or profile page denotes how many people are following you. Click on the number to see who they are.

Following The people you follow. Click on the number on your home page or profile page to see a list of them.

FTW For the win.

Handle *See Username.*

Hashalbum A collection of pictures that have been linked to tweets with a specific hashtag.

Hashphrase A string of words made into a hashtag.

Hashtag Any string of uninterrupted letters or numbers that begins with #. Hashtags automatically become links – click on one and you'll get a timeline of tweets that include it. They're handy if you want to follow everything that's being said about a particular subject. Anyone can make a new one, but users generally settle on one or two hashtags quickly and organically.

Home page The page that automatically loads when you log in to Twitter.

Home timeline A list of tweets by people you follow, organised in reverse chronological order. These are the tweets that automatically appear when you log into your account.

IMO In my opinion.

Impact A measure of how much people talk about you in the Twittersphere, but it also takes into account how many followers you have and how much you interact with others. Expressed as a percentage, 100 means you're very impactful, while 0 means you're not at all. Various companies produce these analyses: figures from Twitalyzer.com are quoted in this book.

Influence A measure of how influential you are over other Twitter users. Simply having lots of followers doesn't make you influential – people have to retweet or mention you. Influence is usually expressed as a percentage, 100 being very influential and 0 not at all. Twitalyzer.com provided the data for this book.

Listed A link on your profile page that shows how many people have included you in a list.

Lists Collections of feeds that individual users have created. You can create your own lists – one way is to go through your profile page and click on the Links tab. You can also follow other people's lists, which you'll find on their profile pages, without also following the users listed in them.

LMAO Laughing my ass off.

INTRO

POLITICS & CURRENT AFFAIRS

ROYALTY & RELIGION

CELEBRITY

SCIENCE & NATURE

SPORT & LEISURE

ARTS, CULTURE & MEDIA

A TWEET A DAY

GLOSSARY & THANKS

INTRO

POLITICS &
CURRENT AFFAIRS

ROYALTY &
RELIGION

CELEBRITY

SCIENCE &
NATURE

SPORT &
LEISURE

ARTS, CULTURE
& MEDIA

A TWEET A DAY

GLOSSARY
& THANKS

LOL Laughing out loud.

Mentions Refers to the section on your home page that lets you see messages where anyone has referenced your Twitter handle. Depending on your settings, these may be visible in a section called @[username]. *See also @.*

Messages *See Direct messages.*

MT Modified tweet. Occasionally used to denote a retweet that's been edited back.

Profile page Your page on the Twitter website, which shows your own timeline, plus information such as how many followers they have. Click on your Twitter handle or the Profile link to get here. If you click on another user's handle, you'll end up on their profile page.

Promoted tweets and hashtags Tweets or hashtags that businesses pay to have put at the top of search results on Twitter.

Protected A Twitter account that the user wants to keep private; to follow you will need the user's permission. To protect your own tweets go to Settings on your home page.

Reply *See @Reply.*

Retweet (RT) (vb & n) To repeat another user's tweet, or the repeat itself. By retweeting someone else's tweet, it will appear in your timeline, just as your tweets would.

On Twitter's website, there is no longer a quick option to edit the tweet before retweeting it with your own comment, but this option still exists in other interfaces, such as Tweetdeck. If you choose to do that, it's customary to put your comment before the text of the retweet, and no quotation marks are necessary. An edited retweet usually looks like this: "GET THE WOMAN SOME TOAST. RT @BreakingNews Update on Gabrielle Giffords' recovery: eating; has made enough speech progress to ask for toast".

Click on the Retweets tab to see retweets by you and others, and which of your own tweets have been retweeted.

ROFL Rolling on the floor laughing.

RT Retweet.

Settings Tools that allow you to manage your Twitter page. Click on your Twitter handle in the top right corner of the home page to find this section. Here, you can alter details about your account, change the look of your profile page and so on. If you like, you can also make your tweets private.

Social network A website designed to allow people to interact. Facebook, MySpace and Google+ are all social networks, as, of course, is Twitter.

Timeline List of tweets sent by any one user. *See also Home timeline.*

TMI Too much information.

Trends *See Trending topics.*

Trending topics The most popular subjects being discussed on Twitter at any one time, although the data is carefully calibrated to show only topics that have recently risen in popularity (otherwise Justin Bieber would constantly clog up the top 10). You can adjust this to show trending topics in different places around the world.

Tweeple, Tweeps People on Twitter.

Tweet (vb & n) To send or post a message, or the message itself (the latter is also known as an Update). An ordinary tweet can be read by anybody. If you'd prefer only your followers to read them, you can make them all private. To do this go to Settings on your home page.

Tweeter Anyone who tweets.

INTRO

POLITICS & CURRENT AFFAIRS

ROYALTY & RELIGION

CELEBRITY

SCIENCE & NATURE

SPORT & LEISURE

ARTS, CULTURE & MEDIA

A TWEET A DAY

GLOSSARY & THANKS

INTRO

POLITICS &
CURRENT AFFAIRS

ROYALTY &
RELIGION

CELEBRITY

SCIENCE &
NATURE

SPORT &
LEISURE

ARTS, CULTURE
& MEDIA

A TWEET A DAY

GLOSSARY
& THANKS

Tweetiest A point at which Twitter was particularly busy. This can be measured, for example, through the volume of tweets per second.

Twibute A tweet written in tribute to someone.

Twidow, twidower Someone whose partner is constantly on Twitter.

Twitpic A separate organisation from Twitter, created to provide an easy way of linking to pictures in tweets. (You can also upload pictures direct to Twitter by clicking on the camera symbol that appears when you start writing a tweet.)

Twitter The website and the company itself, but some people also use the term to mean their Twitter feed.

Twitter feed *See Feed.*

Twitter handle *See Username.*

Twitterati The Twitter elite, denoted either by number of followers or influence.

Twitterer Less common synonym for User or Tweeter.

Twitterverse Everyone on Twitter.

Update Any message posted on Twitter; also known as a Tweet.

User Any individual or group with a Twitter account.

Username The name a user chooses to be called on Twitter; also known as a 'handle'.

Verified account An account, usually of a high-profile tweeter, confirmed by Twitter as genuine (as opposed to a fan or parody). The status is indicated by a tick next to their name.

Who to follow A link that allows you to search by subject for suggestions of users you might be interested in.

INTRO

POLITICS &
CURRENT AFFAIRS

ROYALTY &
RELIGION

CELEBRITY

SCIENCE &
NATURE

SPORT &
LEISURE

ARTS, CULTURE
& MEDIA

A TWEET A DAY

GLOSSARY
& THANKS

— Thanks —

This book was a genuinely collaborative effort, starting with the initial idea, which I would love to claim for my own but which was in fact the brainwave of my friend and very clever editor at Bloomsbury, Alexa von Hirschberg, who told me about it over dinner one night in early July, thereby setting in motion the craziest two months of my life. I could not have done it without Natasha Fairweather, who guided me through the process, and Homa Rastegar Driver and Donald Winchester at AP Watt; my tireless research assistant Chloe Mac Donnell; Anna Simpson, Alexandra Pringle, Laura Brooke, Henry Jeffreys, Paul Nash, Hannah Temby, Benjamin Adams, Laura Keefe and Peter Miller at Bloomsbury; Trish Burgess and Justine Taylor; Jonathan Baker at Seagull Design; Rachel Bremer and Jillian West at Twitter; and Akane Nakamura, Sandra Waehler, Louisa Winkler and Xa Shaw-Stewart who kindly provided translations. I also owe a debt to the perennial early adopter @carolyn_w, who talked me into signing up in the first place, to Joel McIver who gave me great advice and to many of my Twitter friends who gave me invaluable leads, including @mattsimpson23, @meejahoar, @jfkwoodgreen, @LDLDN, @TootyMcFrooty, @HungryHollowaii, @kaybar007, @davisisms and @PayneKate.

I spoke to dozens of social media experts in the making of this book, who were full of help and enthusiasm: Eric T. Peterson at Twitalyzer.com, Jorg Ruis at TwitterCounter.com, Meredith Klee at Topsy.com, Wayne St Amand at CrimsonHexagon.com, Mark Ghuneim and Jason Damata at Trendrr.com, Jen Charlton at Peoplebrowsr.com and ReSearch.ly, Adam Schoenfeld at SimplyMeasured.com and RowFeeder.com, Liz Pullen and Paul Colton at WhatTheTrend.com, Chris McCroskey at TweetCongress.org, David Swaebe at Mullen.com, Sarah Carver at Radian6.com, Sam Yagan at OKCupid.com, Jonathan Pirc at Lab42.com, Cornelia Carter-Sykes at Pew Research Center's Internet & American

INTRO

POLITICS & CURRENT AFFAIRS

ROYALTY & RELIGION

CELEBRITY

SCIENCE & NATURE

SPORT & LEISURE

ARTS, CULTURE & MEDIA

A TWEET A DAY

GLOSSARY & THANKS

Life Project, the Pew Research Center's Project for Excellence in Journalism, Yoh Kawano at UCLA, Ben Kessler at SeatGeek.com, Kirsten Forsberg at WaggenerEdstrom.com, Avishnay Livne and Eytan Adar of the University of Michigan, Ann Arbor, Giles Palmer at Brandwatch.com, Jenn at TweetReach.com, Gawker.com, Mashable.com, Alex Halavais of AoIR.org, Danah.org, Professor Axel Bruns at Queensland University of Technology, Hope Frank of Webtrends, Tokyohive.com, 6theory.com, Klout.com and Alex Nunns and Nadia Idle, editors of *Tweets from Tahrir*.

On a personal note, I'd like to thank my husband, Robin McIver, who cooked dinner every night while I worked upstairs, and my friends and family, who barely saw me all summer.

My biggest debt of gratitude, of course, goes to all of those brilliant writers whose tweets are included in this book. Many, unfortunately, were lost to the cutting room floor, but I want to thank everyone I spoke to in the process of putting it together, from politicians to celebrities to members of the public: your positivity and best wishes made this a great experience from beginning to end.

@1nf1d3IC4str0, @1rick, @20perlz08, @3arabawy, @42nd_Tweet, @666forsatan, @abcgrandstand, @abcnews, @ABCtech, @acarvin, @ACBreakingNews, @ActuallyNPH, @adamwmoore, @AdweekEmma, @AfghanNews24, @afneil, @africamedia_cpj, @Aggersashes, @agirl, @ahmed, @aianucci, @aiww, @ajc AJC, @AlbertoContador, @AlEnglish, @Alex_Kay_DM, @alex_willis , @alexbracken, @alexispetridis, @alexmassie, @Ali_Stephenson_, @aliceemross, @AliDahmash, @Aliesbati, @aliesbati, @Allen_Park, @AlOraibi, @aluvious, @alya1989262, @aman_tyagi, @amiralx, @AmoreBautista, @AndersonCooper, @andre_crow, @Andre_p_Griffin, @AndrewBreitbart, @AndrewMaleMojo, @andrewwander, @andyhaynesed, @andytwood, @AngieCrouch, @AngryBritain, @AnnCurry, @AntDeRosa, @AnthonyQuintano, @antlanelondon, @AP @AP_NFL, @ApocalypseHow, @AriMelber, @Arsenal_Away, @arthurascii, @arusbridger, @ArwaCNN, @asa_wire, @astro_rex, @astro_ron, @astro_sandy, @astro_satoshi, @astroboh, @atk97b, @AussieEllenFans, @B_Hay, @badbanana, @bairdjulia, @barackobama, @BarbaraGSerra, @baseballcrank, @bayfox_1, @bbc24, @bbcbreaking, @BBCPeterHunt, @BBCWorld, @BeardOfBrian, @BeerKat, @BenjaminEdmonds, @bennie_james, @bestbells, @BettyFckinWhite, @biebercruz, @BieberFansFL,

@BieberTeamNY, @BigBoi, @BigShowFactoids, @Billboarddotcom,
@billhuizenga, @BillKempin, @BillMC7, @billybragg, @billyeichner,
@BinkleyOnStyle, @blacknerd, @Blaiseplant, @bnu, @bola_adeyemi76,
@borowitzreport, @BreakingNews, @brenbeers, @BrennanLA, @Brian070,
@brianedwardsmed, @BrisbaneTimes, @BronxZoosCobra, @brunodecock,
@bsebti, @bumbledot, @buzzfeed, @bychrisjenkins, @Bynickdavies,
@CadelOfficial, @cairotango, @Caissie, @caitieparker, @caitlinmoran,
@caitnightjokes, @CalPerryAJ, @CamanPour, @cancrime, @carelpedre,
@CarlBildt, @carlmaxim, @carolinecheese, @CatholicNewsSvc, @CBSNews,
@Chaglen, @channel4news, @CharlesMBlow, @CherylKerl, @chris_
jenkins34, @Chris_Shallow, @ChrisBeanland, @ChrisBryantMP, @chriscolfer,
@cibriddon, @clarebalding1, @ClarenceHouse, @cmendler, @cnnbrk,
@Colmogorman, @ConanOBrien, @CondeElevator, @copystone,
@corybooker, @cpinck, @CrazyColours, @Cristiano and Creative Artists
Agency, @CroweJam, @Cshirky, @Cyrenaican, @daddy_san, @daffodilfairy,
@dakelso, @DalaiLama, @Danekane, @Daniel_Boerman, @danielgene,
@danielmaier, @dankanemitsu, @DannySeesIt, @DarrenRovell, @darthvader,
@dat_Uschi, @davecaughey, @DavidCampbell73, @davidvitty,
@Davidwearing, @db, @DeathStarPR, @delrayser, @der_bluthund,
@derekblasberg, @dgoneill, @diamondgeezer, @DianainHeaven,
@DiscoDebMKE, @DishofSalt, @DitaVonTeese, @Divine_Miss_Em,
@dominicwaghorn, @DominicWaghorn, @domknight, @DonaldGlover,
@dougsaunders, @DrSamuelJohnson, @drunkhulk, @DuwayneBooks,
@Dylanjonesgq, @dzabriskie, @ebertchicago, @Ed_Miliband, @ed_vincent,
@edyong209, @elaineronson, @ElBaradei, @eleanormorgan, @elkgirl,
@elliottyamin, @EmiMarKerr, @empiremagazine, @Eric_Edholm, @ericanhk,
@ericasfish, @EvanHD, @evgenymorozov, @FakeChileans, @FatJew,
@Fieldproducer, @Financial24, @FionnDavenport, @fivethirtyeight,
@Flaneur, @fluffythecat, @flyingperonis, @ForeignOffice, @fortunefunny,
@foster208, @fotofobe, @Frankie_Wah, @FrankRGardner, @Friedmanjon,
@fuggirls, @funnyhumour, @gabmeister1855, @GarethAveyard,
@GeekToMe, @Gene_Cowan47, @GeorgeTakei, @georgiethompson,
@GeraintThomas86, @ghincapie, @Ghonim Wael, @ghostpanther,
@GiulianaRancic, @GlastoFest, @GlobalGrind, @God, @God_Damn_
Batman, @GOOD, @GovBeebeMedia, @GovMikeHuckabee, @Graceisabel,
@grahamsalisbury, @grazia_live, @greatdismal, @guardianeco,
@GuardianUSA, @GuidoFawkes, @H4T, @HalaGorani, @hanniep,
@Happyten, @Has_bookpushers, @HawkinsJT, @HeardinLondon,
@helbobwhitaker, @Heyessa, @Hhartz, @HoeZaay, @HolyGod,

POLITICS & CURRENT AFFAIRS

ROYALTY & RELIGION

CELEBRITY

SCIENCE & NATURE

SPORT & LEISURE

ARTS, CULTURE & MEDIA

A TWEET A DAY

GLOSSARY & THANKS

INTRO

POLITICS &
CURRENT AFFAIRS

ROYALTY &
RELIGION

CELEBRITY

SCIENCE &
NATURE

SPORT &
LEISURE

ARTS, CULTURE
& MEDIA

A TWEET A DAY

GLOSSARY
& THANKS

@howardkurtz, @HRHDukeOfEdin, @HRHPrincessKate,
@HuffingtonPost, @iamMarkRonson, @ianinegypt, @IndiaKnight,
@IranNewsNow, @Ircpresident, @Iskwew, @ITN, @itsmywayrob,
@IvanCNN, @jack, @jackbauer, @jaidaarab, @jakob_fuglsang, @jakob_
fuglsang, @JamesPMorrison, @jamiefahey1, @JaneGrazia, @JarettSays,
@jasonjwilde, @jasonmustian, @jaurosen_nyu, @jaytroyy, @Jcexplorer,
@Jdierkes, @Jedshepherd, @jellison22, @jemima_khan, @Jemmdepaula,
@jeremyscahill, @Jess_Stam, @JessC_M, @JesseCFriedman, @jessejofficial,
@JewAmerPrincess, @jiffywild, @JimBarrowman, @jimgeraghty,
@JKChavanne, @jo_elvin, @joan_rivers, @johnboehner, @JohnLegend,
@johnmonks, @johnnyminkley, @johnprescott, @Jojo_Wu, @jonnelledge,
@JonnieMarbles, @jonsnowC4, @Jordansekulow, @jorgenbp, @josanphoto,
@josephjyoung, @joshgerstein, @joshgroban, @JoshMalina, @joshthomas87,
@joshuaferris, @joshuagates, @josieensor, @joyreidtvnz, @JPBarlow,
@jperrotto, @JFRobertsF1, @jstrevino, @jt_sloosh, @Julian_Ass, @K8TXX,
@KAKA, @kalena, @kamalahmed1, @Karen_DaviLa, @kathviner,
@KatieCouric, @KatyKatopodis, @katyperry, @Keetredkid,
@KeithKirkwood1, @keithurbahn, @kenmogi, @kerryparnell,
@ketilbstensrud, @Kevin_Maguire, @KhloeKardashian, @kierenmccarthy,
@KimKardashian, @kimberleyhalkett, @KimJongil, @kimmar, @kingsthings,
@Kirstymalcolm, @kiwiskivi, @Knifework, @kodyfrazier, @krishgm,
@KrisHumphries, @kyotofoodie, @LadyGaga, @LaJornada, @lancearmstrong,
@larrysabato, @laurencebooth, @LaurenLaverne, @Laurennmcc,
@laurenstendam, @leahburdick, @LebaneseJ, @LeeLloyd66, @leenarao,
@LeighHolmwood, @LeviLeipheimer, @lgolborne, @Liberationtech,
@libyan4life, @life, @lileeny, @liltunechi, @lindacolsh, @lindseyhilsum,
@Lisahendrix, @Lisaling, @lisaskynews, @LiterallyJamie, @liuxia64,
@livwalkeryorks, @loadedsanta, @londontonight, @LoniLove, @Lord_
Voldemort7, @Lordhunt, @LoreleiKing, @LorraineELLE, @LouiseMensch,
@louisedash, @Lukejcr, @maddow, @MaddowBlog, @MagicJohnson,
@makiwi, @MandyGill, @manuelquinziato, @ManzanitaGrunge,
@Mariellaf1, @MarinaHyde, @MarinaMetro, @MarkKnoller,
@MarkCavendish, @MarkHoppus, @markos, @markrenshaw, @martin_nz,
@MartinBrunt, @MartinFitz, @MartinSLewis, @martyn_williams,
@marykissel, @marytwocats, @Matt_Alt, @mattbinder, @Mattcooke_UK,
@MatthewWells, @mattround, @maxwalterssport, @McCain_on_NFL,
@mchancecnn, @mdowney, @MeetJamesFranco, @melissakchan,
@MelissaTweets, @meropemills, @metoffice, @mfullilove, @miafreedman,
@MichalelWolffNYC, @michellemalkin, @migueljmoran, @mike2600,

@MikeDrucker, @MikePasseri, @mikestaszel, @millarmind, @miller_cricket, @MissKatiePrice, @MissRaChilli, @missvmoss, @misterseansd, @mkanders, @mmFlint, @monaeltahawy, @monaeltahawy, @Monasosh, @morafi, @MrBlakeway, @mrfcj, @mrjoezee, @MrPointyHead, @mrssosbourne, @mrsstephenfry, @mrstevegribbin, @Ms_Dynamite, @Mslulurose, @msnbc, @msxmasbaby, @mulegirl, @mydailyuk, @MyNameisRazzle, @Naly_D, @NASA, @natasharenee, @Natwivity, @NevSchulman, @news_va_en, @NewsFromAmnesty, @newssoverseas, @NewtGingrich, @nezbleu, @NFL, @Nick_Nolte, @NickiMinaj, @nicolecav1, @Nigelsarbutts, @nolanjourno, @Nora_LUMIERE, @nouriel, @ns_mehdihasan, @Number10Gov, @nytbishop, @nzherald, @nzstuff, @OfficiallyGT, @ohsouthlondon, @Oliverthring, @ollymoss, @Omar_gaza, @OnionSports, @ourmaninabiko, @oxfam, @packers, @paddypower, @PAIGER33, @Pam_nAshes, @PatateVertigo, @PaulLewis, @paulmmace, @PauloCoelho, @paulverhoeven, @pavolk, @PayneKate, @penjenny, @peoplemag, @pepperpaltrow, @Peston, @Peterdrew, @peterlattman, @PeterLattmann, @PGDougSchneider, @philipoconnor, @PhillipAMorton, @PiersMorgan, @Pink, @pitchforkmedia, @plantemily, @pnoony, @poniewozik, @poohugh, @postworldnews, @pourmecoffee, @Prince_James, @princeharrystag, @PrincessEd89, @PrincessKateFTW, @prodnose, @ProfBrianCox, @ProfVolunteer, @Psaffo, @psam, @pwire, @qikipedia, @quantick, @Queen Rania, @Queen_UK, @QPSmedia, @RagehOmaar, @RaGreeneCNN, @rallaf, @RamyRaoof, @RandyJackson, @RaptureHelpDesk, @Ratbanjos, @Reallyvirtual, @RealRobMugabe, @Refugees, @renayaye, @rep_Giffords, @resudox, @Reuters, @reuters_tlw, @RexHuppke, @rgiraldi, @rgoodchild, @Richard Roeper, @richardpbacon, @richardquest, @rickjnewman, @rickmercer, @ricky_martin, @Rihanna, @Rioferdy5, @Riotcleanup, @robbierowantree, @robdelany, @RobReynolds, @RochelleKilliner, @rodfeuer, @rohitbhargava, @rookie2veteran, @ropate, @rorycarroll72, @Rorysmith_tel, @rosannecash, @RoyalBiographer, @RoyalReporter, @royalweddingcnn, @Rtege, @rustyrockets, @RuthieGledhill, @ryanhanrahan, @RyanJL, @RyanSeacrest, @SaeedCNN, @safeinchch, @SageFrancis, @Sai__kun, @SaliWho, @Salliestweets, @salmaeldaly, @SamatRedmag, @SamdeBrito, @samihtoukan, @Sandmonkey, @sandrajapandra, @SantiagoTimes, @sarahbrownuk, @sarahrainey4, @sarasidnercnn, @sasatredmag, @schleckfrank , @sciam, @scottbeibin, @seanoconnz, @sebastianpinera, @security4all, @Selintellect, @serafinowicz, @sgourley, @Shabana_A, @SHAQ, @Sheri_Beri_2112, @Shmula, @SiClancy, @simonlebon, @simonpegg, @SkyMarkWhite,

INTRO

POLITICS &
CURRENT AFFAIRS

ROYALTY &
RELIGION

CELEBRITY

SCIENCE &
NATURE

SPORT &
LEISURE

ARTS, CULTURE
& MEDIA

A TWEET A DAY

GLOSSARY
& THANKS

@skynews, @skynewsbreak, @skynewsgatherer, @SkyNewsPolitics, @Slate, @snivellingpinko, @sockington, @spatouttweets, @Sports_k1ng, @SrinJoy, @steelers, @Steelersdepot , @SteveMartinToGo, @stephenfry and David Higham Associates, @stolethetarts, @Stuffspannsays, @SudanTribuneENG, @SultanAlQassemi, @suntimesbazzaf, @suppuser, @susiebubble, @suzemuse, @swhite_hud, @swirlywand, @T3MagUk, @Tamegoeswild, @tarekshalaby, @TckTckTck, @teamyasumura, @tech2learn, @techcrunch, @Ted_Newton, @TeleFashion, @TelegraphNews, @Terrymoran, @Tharwacolamus, @thatdanstevens, @the_archbishop, @the_topspin, @theAlPitcher, @theashes, @TheEllenShow, @theeMikeV, @TheFuckingPope, @theharryshearer, @TheHoxtonRaj, @TheInDecider, @thelittleidiot, @TheLordYourGod, @theonion, @thepoke, @TheSourceMag, @TheSTStyle, @TheTrout91, @TheTweetOfGod, @ThinkProgress, @thisroughmagic, @THR, @ThurnbsThurnbs, @timcoombs79, @TimGatt, @TJMannixNYC, @tlaquetzqui, @tokyoreporter, @TomokoHosaka, @TonjeVassbotn, @TransitionVert, @Tribrix, @Tvdonewright, @TVGuide, @TweetChina, @TweetMinster, @TweetofSatan, @Twister_Tracker, @TwopTwips, @tyetyeee, @Tyga_YMCMB, @tzarimas, @UK_Blackberry, @Ukuncut, @UN, @ungraceful, @UnRightsWire, @usarsnl, @USWeekly, @Vacuumcleaner, @VancouverSun, @VantageNews, @Vaughancricket, @vegancto, @vichoon, @virginiafoxx, @VirgoBlue, @vodafonenz, @vogue_london, @vozdacomunidade, @wallaceme, @WarGames06, @warne888, @wefeedback, @wendythebee, @Wesstreeting, @Whatleydude, @wikileaks, @willemsfrederik, @Willsh, @windingroad, @wingoz, @wkelly, @Women2Drive, @WorldVisionAus, @wossy, @WSJ, @xsnowwhitestew, @yapdates, @YokoOno, @Zeinobia, @zhoeg and @zodthoughts.

— Sources —

p. 17 Pew Research Center's Project for Excellence in Journalism, 'Social Media Debate a Mortgage Mess, Science and Religion', 11–15 October 2010, http://www.journalism.org/index_report/social_media_debate_mortgage_mess_science_and_religion.

p. 22 Pew Internet & American Life Project, '22% of online Americans used social networking or Twitter for politics in 2010 campaign', 27 January, 2011, http://www.pewinternet.org/Reports/2011/Politics-and-social-media.aspx.

p. 23 'The Party is Over Here: Structure and Content in the 2010 Election', Avishay Livne, Matthew P. Simmons, Eytan Adar, Lada A. Adamic; University of Michigan, Ann Arbor, 2011, http://www.cond.org/partyat.pdf.

p. 27 Pew Research Center's Project for Excellence in Journalism, 'A Special Report on the Media and the Tucson Shooting', 10–16 January 2011, http://www.journalism.org/index_report/pej_news_coverage_index_january_1016_2011.

p. 43 Pew Research Center's Project for Excellence in Journalism, 'Twitterers Tackle Murdoch's Tabloid Scandal', 4–8 July 2011, http://www.journalism.org/index_report/twitterers_tackle_murdoch%E2%80%99s_tabloid_scandal.

p. 137 Pew Research Center's Project for Excellence in Journalism, 'Twitter Responds to the Japanese Disaster', March 7–11, 2011, http://www.journalism.org/index_report/twitter_responds_japanese_disaster.

INTRO

POLITICS & CURRENT AFFAIRS

ROYALTY & RELIGION

CELEBRITY

SCIENCE & NATURE

SPORT & LEISURE

ARTS, CULTURE & MEDIA

A TWEET A DAY

GLOSSARY & THANKS